Along the EARLY TRAILS of the Southwest

Illustrated by

Melvin C. Warren 1968

Trail Branding on the King Ranch

along the
EARLY TRAILS
of the
Southwest

by:
Wayne Gard, Dean Krakel,
Joe B. Frantz, Dorman Winfrey,
H. Gordon Frost, Donald Bubar.

Introduction by:
John H. Jenkins

Illustrated by:

Melvin C. Warren

AUSTIN and NEW YORK 1969
THE PEMBERTON PRESS
Jenkins Publishing Company

The CONTENTS

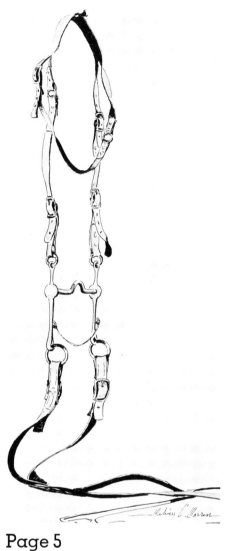

The ILLUSTRATIONS

Melvin Warren, Western Artist

DURING THIS wobegone era in the history of art, where most paintings are unintelligible and nearly all are far beyond the fringe of realism, it is refreshing to come upon an artist whose paintings are realistic, in the good senses of the word, and whose paintings are entirely indigenous to America and the American spirit. This has been the era of the Exercise in art; when one looks at current works one sees experiment—frequently ill-conceived, impromptu, what one might call extemporaneous exercises, a striving for individualism, for the different rather than the beautiful.

In this time of a million would-be artists it has become, so art schools and art critics too often seem to teach, necessary to create a "style," an individual way of painting different from that of any other, to "fulfill the artist's inner needs," to gain recognition or fortune, to interpret mankind and his world, and, more recently, to blow one's mind. It is hardly an era of honest, forthright art.

Melvin C. Warren of Texas is helping to refocus our attention on natural beauty as at least one legitimate goal of art, and is doing so, it happens, with realistic paintings of the American Southwest.

To Warren beauty is not the fadish or the stylish. He does not proclaim his preference for realism to be the only true way to beauty in art. He merely shows it to be one authentic way, and certainly his way. Just as with James Joyce's *Ulysses* and Mark Twain's *Tom Sawyer,* one can only choose a path to beauty best suited to himself. If either Carl Sandburg in his preference for *Tom Sawyer* or Arthur Miller in his preference for *Ulysses* mocked the other, both would be wrong. Nothing is more sickening than to see a would-be critic parrot praises over some current exercise in technique and then say "Frederic who?" when shown a fine Remington oil.

Warren was born in Los Angeles, March 19, 1920, and moved as a child with his family from ranch to ranch, residing in California, Arizona, New Mexico, and Texas, settling on a Seymour, Texas, ranch in 1934. Moved by the variety of landscape of the Southwest and by the vitality of the life of the ranchers, cowmen, rodeo riders, and horse trainers, and by the tales of the oldtimers, Warren began to paint and sketch, certainly without thought of selling or profit, only a keen need for an outlet for the images and emotions brought on by the scenes about him. It was not long, of course, before he was bitten by the bug: upon entering a bakery with a painting under his arm during the lean depression years, he was met with a proposal to trade the painting for five dollars credit on bread. At the risk of a terrible pun, painting has been his bread and butter ever since.

In 1941 Warren married, then joined the air force, serving four full years. After the war he and his wife Lucille moved to Fort Worth and he entered art school at Texas Christian University. There he found an unusual professor, Samuel P. Ziegler, who taught well and at the same time let Warren's natural abilities develop along the path they were destined to follow. Warren received his fine arts degree in 1952.

Seldom has a more sincere and unassuming man entered the world of art. Unclad in smock or beret, without beard, mustache, or female-length hair, non-protesting, non-pacifist, non-communist, non-radical, Melvin C. Warren directs his time and attention fifty hours a week to his proper calling: the painting of beautiful pictures. Since he does not toy around with his calling, his production is only three or four a month.

Warren's ideas come before he starts painting—a natural order, unfortunately relatively unknown in New York art circles—and many hours are spent in his studio sitting before the blank canvas. When he has his plan well in mind there is little need for elaborate preliminary sketches. His tendency is towards umbers and siennas; he prefers reds, yellows, and earth colors.

Much of Warren's time is spent roaming the

Southwest, not only seeing but renewing his rapport with the land and its peculiar beauties. He is not a "repeat" painter, and each canvas, while recognizable from afar as a Warren, has a startling freshness of subject matter without disturbing the same central theme. This desire for new subject matter has led Warren across thousands of miles of Texas, New Mexico, Arizona, California, Oklahoma, and Wyoming landscape on horseback, in jeeps and nowadays in a Volkswagen camper-bus.

Melvin C. Warren is making a place for himself as one of America's great artists, and doing so in an era catageorically opposed to his subject matter and style. His progress in the face of this opposition is a pleasant and rewarding experience for those of us who know his genius.

John H. Jenkins

The Butterfield Overland Mail Trail
by **DORMAN H. WINFREY**

Illustrations by:
Melvin C. Warren

Melvin C Warren 1987

AMONG THE legendary institutions of the American West, few have come to characterize its spirit so well as the Butterfield Overland Mail. We remember it in story and legend for the vision and daring of its founders, and for the indomitable courage of the men who, guiding galloping horses and swaying coaches, prevailed against deserts and mountains, Indians and thirst. Time has now dimmed our memories and added to history the luster of nostalgic imagination; we see in our mind's eye not what was, but what, it seems to us, should have been. This is the fate of history. The Butterfield Mail was indeed the product of the finest qualities of the men of its day and of the nation. That is what it means to us. But it was much else besides, and has another meaning as well. For it was also the product of what was less admirable—of the short-sightedness, self-seeking, and intolerance that marked its era, as they do all eras.

The human race fancies that in the conduct of

its affairs it sets aside those petty prejudices and visionary dreams which dominate the lesser sphere of individuals' lives, and ascends to a higher realm where objective judgments and clear vision hold sway. In this it more often than not flatters its own vanity, for it is not in man to suspend his nature. A large part of that nature is the tendency to respond to the uncertain or unknown with the creation of legend. Man, perhaps, could not bear the "shock of recognition" of the reality of his human situation without the protective shields of legend and dream. Thus it is that his myths determine what he thinks a situation is as much as does reality, and it is to them that he most often responds when dealing with his world.

Chief among the ideas which dominated mid-nineteenth century America was what Frederick Jackson Turner called "a geography of public opinion." Sectional awareness touched every major issue of the age, and the most distinctive and the most powerful of its myths was that of the great western frontier and of the "Manifest Destiny"—or as one historian more aptly called it, Manifest Desire—of the nation to embrace it politically. Expansionism was in the air; the dream of nineteenth century America was of the west, of gold to be discovered and of virgin soil to be tilled. From 1844 to the outbreak of the Civil War, the acquisition of new territory dominated politics, as California, Texas, Kansas, and Oregon, opened to Americanization.

Intruding upon this myth and giving it a distinctive cast was yet another, which would distort mere sectional awareness into a self-conscious and defensive parochialism. That was slavery, the "peculiar institution" of the south. The realities of its existence and what it meant to the nation were veiled behind a self-righteous pose in both north and south, where both confused right with righteous and wrong with wicked, so that ultimately they found themselves unable to compromise—for one does not compromise with the devil. When the question of slavery was injected into the dream of the frontier, expansion ceased to be a question merely of peopling and adopting into the Union the western lands. Now, as it had been the manifest destiny of the nation to expand its government throughout the length and breadth of the west, so it became the destiny of both the north and south to see her sons capture the prize, not for the nation, but for their myth. To the south, the west offered an opportunity to expand the geographical limits of slavery, and thus to increase the representation and influence of the pro-slavery states in the Congress. To the north, it was a hope for an expanded region of freedom. Other factors were influential, but, as the myth of slavery cast its shadow over every major national question of the age, so it came to dominate the government's frontier policies.

The establishing of the Butterfield Overland Mail was a product of such dreams, and a foil in the duel that raged about the fallacies of sectional thinking. Though there were very real economic and political factors which were felt to require its establishment, even stronger than the need for an overland mail was the desire for it, and this was the offspring of the popular legend of the Great West and its

20

destiny as a part of the Union.

Neither the need nor the desire for an overland mail was new as the decade of the '50's opened, but rather they were culmination of a series of factors that had been building to a climax over a long period of time. Although California would not come into the Union until 1850, she already had by that time a population of over 200,000, composed chiefly of immigrants from the United States, and there was a desire on both sides to maintain communication. In the 1840's and 1850's there was a sudden spurt of settlement of the west coast, as the ending of the Mexican War in 1848, the Gadsden Purchase, and particularly the discovery of gold offered incentives to the great wave of immigrants that descended on California. Those who moved to the continent's further shores could not easily break their bonds with the country they had left. A contemporary traveler observing the nature of the western immigrants, wrote, "Congregate a hundred Americans beyond the settlements, and they immediately lay out a city, form a State constitution and apply for admission to the union, while twenty-five of them become candidates for the United States Senate." These displaced citizens maintained a ceaseless clamor for an efficient system of mail service with the homes they had left behind.

Further pressures on the government to open communications with the west came from traders and merchants who wished to establish commercial communication with northern Mexico, California, and Santa Fe. To those in the north especially, the West seemed an unlimited market, where profits awaited the clever trader and exploiter. Land speculators, town builders, ferry tenders, tavern keepers, lumbermen, and a score of others saw a vast opportunity to make money.

The feasibility of opening trade routes had already been adequately demonstrated, both through the travels of immigrants and through a series of surveying expeditions which the government had sent into the west since 1848. These surveys were undertaken for various reasons, chiefly to establish the necessity and desirability of military posts, but also to locate suitable roads for immigrants, traders, and other travelers. And always in the back of everyone's mind was the coming of the railroads to the west and their need for suitable roads.

In 1849 the government had sponsored seven reconnaissance tours through Texas, and in 1852 and 1853 a number of surveys were made which established several possible routes across Texas. In 1852 Major William H. Emory led a reconnaissance of the Big Bend country, and his recommendations led to the establishment of a line of military forts along his route, beginning with Fort Davis in 1854. The Army appropriation bill of 1853 was amended specifically to provide for railroad surveys across the southern territory. Five routes were to be explored and mapped out. This Pacific Railroad Survey, and especially the routes taken by Captains Randolph B. Marcy and John Pope, was to form the chief defense of the southern route across the continent. And the report of John R. Bartlett, U. S. Boundary Commissioner from 1850-53 in connection with the negotations for the Gadsden Purchase, substantiated the findings of the military surveyors. Thus, while government explorations of the west were carried out for several purposes, only one of which was to encourage trade and settlement by finding routes west—they in fact demonstrated to the nation the feasibility of crossing the continent and increased the demand for immediate actions toward that goal.

The desire for communication with the West Coast was not limited to a mail service; in fact, it was secondary to the dream of a railroad line stretching across the continent. In the nineteenth century there was a romantic facination with the railroad, not only for the great roaring locomotives themselves, but for the promise they held of a means of conquering the remotest stretches of the American continent. The era of railroad expansion throughout the country was just beginning, and the ultimate conquest of the iron horse was the extension of its lines to the Pacific. One of the chief purposes of the Gadsden Purchase of 1853 had been the acquisition of a viable railroad route across the continent; it added 29,670 square miles of southern territory to the expanding nation.

During the fifties the possibility of obtaining railroad communication with the west was on everyone's mind; not only the economic motives of the railroad companies themselves, but the expansionist visions of the entire population were focused on the vehicle of the railroads as a means of turning its dreams to reality. The second session of the thirty-second Congress, meeting in 1852 and 1853 gave more time and attention to the subject of a transcontinental railroad than to any other, and in 1853 a bill was actually introduced to authorize the construction of a railroad from San Francisco with branches to various sections of the country. This measure failed, but the fact that the government gave consideration to entering the railroad business itself was indicative of the compelling temper of the country.

What turned the eyes of those wishing to establish communication with the west to the setting up of mail routes specifically was the realization that it offered a means of binding that section more closely to the eastern culture its immigrants had left behind. Senator Seward expressed the prevailing opinion when he said, "I regard the inland postal system as a great instrumentality for maintaining, preserving and extending this Union." An overland mail route was seen as a means of opening up the west to easy access to immigrants. "Nothing can so quickly open the land routes as the regular running of mail and passenger stages," wrote a California newspaper. With the routes established by the mail line, it continued, travellers would have "no uncertainty about the road; no fear of scarcity of grass; no dread of a famine or death from thirst. They will move along like tartar or gypsies, feeling perfect security, knowing that they will reach the end of their journey in the course of time, and viewing their journey rather as an occasion of frolic and enjoyment." Such journalistic hyperbole, rampant throuqh the nation, intensified the qeneral conviction that the western movement required an overland mail. This was the prevailing sentiment, except that in the south it came to mean more specifically the extension of proslavery territory into the west. It meant a new section to be populated by slaveholders or their sympathizers and a consequent increased representation in the Congress. The railroads too, encouraged the establishment of a mail route as a trail blazer, especially the Missouri-Pacific, which had definite plans for building to the west; the mail would pave the way for the railroads, not only in marking the best routes west, but in improving them also at government expense.

A second major argument in favor of the establishment of an overland mail line was the relative slowness and inefficiency of the current mail service, which was carried largely by ship from New York to San Francisco. The first official mail service to the Pacific Coast was a steamship service, established on March 3, 1847. It was designed largely as a means of furnishing an adjunct to the U. S. Navy in case of need at a minimum cost to the government. The act, "providing for the Building and Equipment of four Naval Steamships," had for its purpose the construction of ships which could be converted to war duty, and made it the task of the Secretary of the Navy to contract for transporting the mails by these ships between New York and Chagres, Panama, twice monthly each way.

The object of the law is evident in the specifications for the ships, which were rather excessive for mere postage vessels. They were to be a minimum of fifteen tons with 1000 horsepower engines, and were to be constructed under the superintendence of the Navy Department. Furthermore, they were to be commanded by officers of the United States Navy and under Navy control, and the Government was to have the right to requisition them at any time subject to compensation of the contractors. The maximum sum appropriated for this contract was to be $290,000 yearly. An additional contract was specified to run from Panama to Oregon Territory, once each month each way. Three steamers and monthly service were to be provided, at a figure of $199,000 per year.

Complying with the law, the Secretary of the Navy contracted with A. G. Sloo of Ohio to transport the mail from New York to Chagres and with Arnold Harris of Arkansas for service from Panama to Astoria, both contracts of ten years' duration. Both of these men then transferred their contracts, Sloo to three men who agreed to construct two steamships for service by October 1, 1849. When the ships were not completed on time, a "temporary arrangement" to use "inferior vessels" was accepted, and service was begun in December, 1848.

The Panama to Oregon contract was transferred to William H. Aspinwall on November 19, 1847, to be effective for ten years from October, 1848. To accomplish this the Pacific Mail Steamship Company was incorporated in April 12, 1848, and constructed three vessels. Service was begun October 6, 1848. The ships of this company provided fairly regular service, and until 1858 they were the mail link between the pioneers and gold hunters in the west and the east. Other companies arose, but were forced out or bought out by the government subsidized enterprize.

The volume of mail west via the ocean service was large—in 1850 an average of 30,000 letters per month were carried by ship. The first postage rate to the Pacific Coast had been set in March of 1847 at forty cents for a single letter; in 1851 when postage rates were generally reduced, the charge dropped to six cents, and in 1855 they were again raised to ten cents. It was not the charge, however, which aroused the most public criticism, but rather the poor public service that the steamships provided. The Pacific Mail Steamship Company and United States Mail Steamship were viewed as a monopoly charging excessive prices and giving poor service, so that even in Congress it was argued that the breaking of the monopoly would be a major benefit of an overland line.

Chiefly, however, the founding of an overland mail service was looked to as a means of binding the Pacific Coast to the Union, to "prevent the possibility of the future establishment of a separate nation beyond the Sierras," and to offer the east the advantages of trading with it. The carrying of the mail overland was not the sole concern of those in the East, however; in California and the other territories of the west, it was looked upon as a necessary step toward the prosperity and safety of the region. California, in 1856, was so concerned about the question that she sent a petition to Congress asking for construction of wagon roads into her borders, a preliminary toward eventual mail routes. This huge document contained 75,000 signatures, and it had its effect—in 1857, Congress made appropriations for four roads to that State.

The year before California's Senator Weller had introduced a bill authorizing construction of "two bridged and fortified wagon roads to California; one from Independence, Missouri, to San Francisco by way of South Pass, Salt Lake City, and the Humboldt River; the other from El Paso to Los Angeles over the Gila Trail route" and this was the proposal that was adopted. The provision for roads over both northern and southern routes, energetically championed by Senator Thomas J. Rusk of Texas, offered a more or less acceptable compromise between north and south, and largely for this reason it passed. The northern road received an appropriation of $300,000 "for improvement of overland transportation," while the El Paso-Los Angeles road received $200,000. The bill specified that each route should, in addition to general improvements toward smoother roads, have established wells, cavalry posts, and freight depots.

In May of 1857 operations of the El Paso road began under the direction of James B. Leach, who was made superintendent of construction. Leach's road was to extend from El Paso to Fort Yuma, and when he had completed his task, it was eighteen feet wide on straight stretches, and twenty-five feet wide on curves, and had been largely cleared of timber, brush, rocks, and steep grades. The existence of this already fairly satisfactory road was to become yet another argument for putting a mail line on it.

By 1857, some efforts had already been taken in the direction of extending overland mail service to the west, so that a single transcontinental mail line was but a logical step and an already proven possibility. As early as 1846 there was pressure for a transcontinental mail service; in August 5 of that year President James K. Polk in a message to Congress recommended the establishment of a mail service between East and West.

Until 1848 overland mail travel to the Pacific Coast was almost entirely military; there was little encouragement for private efforts to develop overland passengers, mail, or freight service. In 1848 a military mail was carried by horseback from western and intermediate posts to the east; civilians could use this service; but it did not provide them with regular schedules since it ran at the requirements of the military. Of these military riders, perhaps the most famous is Kit Carson.

This situation changed with the discovery of gold, when a great demand suddenly arose for transportation and communication with the west, and people almost overnight became willing to pay almost any price for them. With the exception of providing for the military, the government before 1850 did not take any vigorous steps toward establishing an overland mail, though under pressure it made a few sporadic efforts. Most early overland enterprises were promoted by private companies, and from 1847 to 1849 there were a number of companies that rose up overnight to carry mail and freight, but especially passengers, to the gold regions. In 1847 a mail route was established from Independence, Missouri, to Santa Fe. Carried by wagon, the mail usually composed part of a train including emigrants and a well armed escort. A monthly service, it was looked on especially as a harbinger of future railroad service.

A different demand for mail service came in 1847, when the Mormons settled in the Great Salt Lake basin. In the absence of a federal mail service, they attempted to provide their own, but in 1849 the United States post office was established at Salt Lake City, and the next year a contract was let to carry the mail to that settlement and Independence, Missouri. This service passed through several contractors by 1857, and as a result it never provided very regular service. In 1851 the Mormons saw a mail route establishing from their city to Placerville, California; and later to Sacramento; in spite of difficulties with weather and Indians, this mail was carried fairly regularly and frequently in less than schedule time. In 1854 its route was changed to travel over the Mormon Trail from Salt Lake City to San Diego. This was a $14,000 contract for a monthly service.

By 1857 it was evident that an overland mail was inevitable and the issue shifted to what route should be chosen to bear the line. There was some opposition to the government's undertaking to underwrite such a vast project as the formation of a single great service to the west coast. This came chiefly from the steamship lines which saw their own service being undercut, and which had considerable political influence. An even stronger source of opposition lay within the Congress itself; there were a number of members who believed that rather than undertaking this new project which would increase the costs of the department tremendously, the Post Office Department should attempt to reduce its expenditures. To those conscious of economy, it seemed that the Post Office Department should attempt to make itself, to whatever extent possible, self-supporting, and that it was not its function to serve as a "pioneering agency, leading the emigration, encouraging settlement, and making safe the routes of travel," but rather strictly to provide efficient mail service with the least possible cost to the government. But the tide of public opinion was against such thinking, and debate on the mail question came to center more and more upon what route the service should take. Except by the economists, it came almost to be an axiom that the Post Office Department should serve temporarily as a "trailblazer of civilization to the west."

There were four major routes under consideration by Congress, and with one exception, they all provided for the transportation of the mails to San Francisco. The northern route started at St. Louis and Independence, Missouri, and was substantially the route that was in use via Salt Lake City.

The Middle Route departed from the city of Springfield, Missouri, and followed the Canadian River to Tejon Pass by way of Albuquerque and Mojave River. Entering California, it passed through the Tulare and San Joaquin valleys via San Jose to San Francisco along the 35th parallel route.

The southern route, or thirty-second parallel route, took a course from St. Louis, Missouri, through Indian Territory and Texas to California. It would become the route of the Butterfield Overland Stage.

The fourth route, known as "Jim Birch's route," was not so truly a transcontinental route as the others, and its main advantage lay in the fact that it was already in operation. The route took its name from the contractor who operated a mail service over it. In 1857 James E. Birch signed a contract for the amount of $150,000 to carry the mail twice a month between San Antonio and San Diego by way of El Paso, allowing thirty days each way for the trip. It began at San Antonio, and passed through the Pecos Valley to the thirty-first parallel, where it took a course through Fort Davis and the Rio Grande valley to El Paso and Fort Fillmore, then taking the thirty-second parallel route to Fort Yuma and San Diego. Known as the San Antonio and San Diego Mail Line, it was supported by Texas, the southern states, and lower California. Birch's was the first contract for service on the southern route, which was used a great deal by immigrants from the south and the southwest.

The awarding of the contract to the San Antonio and San Diego Mail Line was largely an attempt to find a temporary solution to the question of establishing a Pacific Mail route. It was to be a way mail on the extreme southern route pending the granting of the contract for the "Great Overland Mail." Its contract provided for payments of $149,000 per annum for a period of four years. With a route covering 1,476 miles, the company employed 65 men, and owned 50 coaches and 400 mules. It required fifty to sixty days to reach San Francisco using the facilities of the San Antonio—San Diego line "under the most favorable conditions." The San Antonio—San Diego mail was semi-monthly until July, 1858, when it was changed to a weekly service, with an increased compensation to $191,488.

The discussion of the choice of routes soon became a struggle for sectional influence between the pro-slavery advocates of the southern states, and the representatives of the industrial and commercial northeast. The degeneration of the mail question into an acrimonious dispute in which it was a pawn in the power play between north and south was but one in a series of incidents that would ultimately erupt into the Civil War. The acquisitions of new territories had long been a major battleground of sectional factions. The Gadsden Purchase and the treaty of Guadalupe Hidalgo, as well as the annexation of Texas, had all been catalysts to sectional controversy. The Kansas-Nebraska controversy and the bloody Kansas War of 1856 further inflamed a situation that had already become almost unendurable. Now the question of where to establish the main line of communication with the frontier territories renewed the dispute.

The people of the north, more commercially inspired, were willing to accept a southern route if they could also obtain one joining the north to upper California, where most of the gold had been discovered. Above all, the north demanded convenient access from the road to her centers of commerce and industry. California's representatives, meanwhile, insisted on San Francisco as the western terminus of the route. The south, arguing against both, wanted San Diego as the terminus of the west, and a southern city as the eastern end of the line.

The merchants and the antislavery populace of the north demanded a route over the Oregon Trail, crossing the Rocky Mountains. The south wanted a route across the south and Texas, along the Gila Emigrant Trail. Texas, closely tied by bonds of sentiment to the south, followed her lead in insisting on a southern route, and preferred to continue that route which already passed through her territory. On January 29, 1858, her legislature passed a joint resolution that "Our Senators and Representatives in the Congress of the United States, be and are hereby requested to use their efforts to procure the passage of a law establishing a weekly overland mail, from some point in Texas, to San Diego in the State of California, with an appropriation sufficient to enable the contractor or contractors, therefore, to erect suitable stations at convenient points along said route." Its instructions were carried out faithfully, with Texas' members of Congress staunchly defending a mail route through Texas. Sam Houston, most colorful and most influential of Texans in Washington, spoke vigorously in the Senate in favor of it. There was, he told the upper chamber, "no route that can be traveled with the same expedition, with the same advantages, with the same certainty comparable at all seasons of the year, comparable to the route from San

Antonio to San Diego."

The arguments were made the more intense by virtue of the general recognition that the route adopted for the overland mail would be a precursor of the Pacific railroad route, which was strongly wished for by both sections. As early as 1844 conflict on the question of the railroad's location, the north held for a Chicago to San Francisco line, while the south preferred a route from New Orleans, Vicksburg, or Memphis, extended across the southwest to lower California. The north, already possessing a vast network of railroads, wished for the route to be located so as to accommodate easily its extension into the western areas, while the southerners "wanted it so as to accommodate their trade, and, it was alleged by some, in case of a dissolution of the union, to secure California." The latter was not so far-fetched as it may have appeared, for sounds of secession had already been emanating from the south, and the Kansas dispute had supplied ready evidence that southerners were vitally concerned with preserving the territorial equilibrium between free and slave states. The opening of a southern route to carry the mail offered the south an opportunity to maintain close contacts with an already sympathetic people who offered major strategic advantages in the event of a disolution of the union. The population of southern California was chiefly composed of immigrants from the southern states, who, though not slave-holders themselves, were not unkindly disposed toward the south. It was the belief of most southern men that California could be won to the cause of slavery and support for the south "if joined to Texas by means of rapid communication."

Because of the sectional division on the location of the proposed mail route, and because of the intensity of feeling on the question, debate in Congress on the question tended to sarcasm and bitterness, and for a time threatened to result in a deadlock. In 1855-56 no fewer than six bills for the establishment of mail routes to California were introduced, but all failed to pass when the members could not agree on a route to be used. In 1857, however, a solution of a kind was settled on, by taking the responsibility for selecting the exact route out of the hands of Congress and giving it to the Post Office Department. On March 3, 1857, the Post Office Appropriation Bill was passed, with an amendment, the drafting of which was largely led by Thomas J. Rusk of Texas, authorizing the Post Master to accept bids for the opening of a semi-weekly mail service "from some point on the Mississippi River" to San Francisco, California. The sum to be paid for the service was to be from $300,000 to $600,000, depending upon the frequency of the mail schedule, which was to be determined by the Post Master General. The contractor was to provide "good four horse coaches or spring wagons, suitable for the conveyance of passengers as well as the safety and security of the mails," and would have the right of preemption to 320 acres of unclaimed land where required to set up a station. The choice of the eastern terminus of the line was to rest with the contractor, according to the law, but in fact it was determined by the Post Master General through his power to select the contractor. On

September 1, 1857, John Butterfield and associates signed a six year contract for $600,000 per year for a semi-weekly mail service between St. Louis and San Francisco. There were nine bids for the original contract, three of which were submitted by Butterfield, offering alternate routes.

The official name of the company founded by Butterfield and associates to carry out the terms of the contract was "The Overland Mail Company," but it was called by various names in different sections of the country. In Missouri it was the Great Southern Overland, and Californians, somewhat chauvinistically called it the California Overland Express, while elsewhere it was known simply as the Butterfield Line. The men who joined Butterfield in the enterprise were all partners in one or another of the four largest express companies in the United States: Adams, American, National, and Wells Fargo. Although there was much skepticism that they would be able to make an efficient operation of it, certainly there was no group in the country more capable of attempting such a vast undertaking.

Butterfield's first proposal for the route was calculated to give as little offense as possible to either north or south. St. Louis was to be the eastern terminus, and the route was to go "by way of the Santa Fe Trail to New Mexico, and then to California along the thirty-fifth parallel." This route, though chiefly through the southwest, did not run through the "solid south" state of Texas, and for this reason was found objectionable by many southerners, who stood staunchly for such a route. Among these was Post Master Aaron Vail Brown, a Tennessean, who even before the contract was officially let, "suggested to John Butterfield that his firm might be given the contract if Memphis were made the eastern terminus of the line, and the route were southwest through Arkansas to the Red River, across the entire state of Texas to El Paso, and on to California by the road along the Gila Trail."

There were, however, several advantages to the choice of St. Louis as the eastern terminus rather than Memphis; it had direct rail connections with all the large cities of the East, while Memphis had none, and the Missouri-Pacific railroad, building a line across Missouri, had already reached Tipton, one hundred sixty miles west of St. Louis, thus providing a rail auxiliary to the coach service. Butterfield had planned to transport mail over the railroad, starting his coaches from the various railheads as the line extended westward. This would not only reduce his firm's operating expense, it would add to its passenger business, since western Missouri and eastern Kansas were already well-populated. In addition to the more than thirteen railroad lines operating through St. Louis, it also was the center for over seventy steamboat lines, and was the traditional launching place for journeys into the west. Brown, however, was adamant on the use of Memphis as an eastern terminus.

Butterfield then proposed a compromise measure, using two routes, one from St. Louis and one from Memphis, as far as Fort Smith, Arkansas, from which the road "would follow the Marcy-Simpson Trail to El Paso, the newly improved Gila Trail road to Los Angeles, and continue to San Francisco by way of the San Joaquin Valley." Now, however, Brown did not like the choice of Fort Smith, but suggested instead that the roads join at Little Rock. The route he wanted would have deprived the company of virtually any local passenger business, for the only town of any size on the fourteen-hundred mile roadless stretch from Memphis to El Paso was Little Rock itself, and, passing through this "uninhabited wilderness," the line would have been tremendously expensive to equip. A trail run by the Little Rock route demonstrated the impracticability of this choice, after which Brown conceded the choice of the merging of the two roads at Fort Smith. The final settlement upon the route aroused much unfavorable comment, especially from the north and east, which had long viewed Post Master Brown with suspicion, and saw his decision as confirming his favoritism toward the south. The Chicago *Tribune* called it "one of the greatest swindles ever perpetrated upon the country by the slave-holders," and the comment was by no means unique.

The Butterfield line was a merging of old and new routes across the west; where possible it followed established trails for economy and ease of passage, and opened new ones only if such action demonstrably could save time in the running of the coaches. The section of the route from Memphis to Little Rock covered five hundred miles and was made by boat; from Little Rock was another 200 miles by coach to Fort Smith. To expedite the service a semi-weekly passenger, mail, and freight service on the Arkansas River between Fort Smith and Little Rock was opened. The trip from St. Louis to Tipton, the starting place for the coaches of the line, was made by rail.

The population of Fort Smith, Arkansas, in 1857 was about 2500, and it was on the border of the Indian Territory. The stages came here almost directly south from Tipton through the Ozark Mountains and Fayetteville. Joining the mail from Memphis, they crossed southwest through Indian Territory to Colbert's Ferry on the Red River, where they passed into Texas. At Nail's Crossing, the route dropped south to Sherman, then west, passing through Forts Belknap, Griffin, Phantom Hill, and Chadbourne. At Camp Johnston it veered west to Horsehead Crossing, where it turned northwest to follow the Pecos River, paralleling the Marcy Trail from Emigrant's Crossing to Pope's Crossing, where the Butterfield took a course through the Guadalupe Mountains for El Paso. This route lay north of the San Antonio-San Diego Mail Line route until the two routes joined at El Paso and continued over the same road to Fort Yuma.

West from El Paso to Fort Yuma the route was largely without water, except for that provided at at the company's stations. At Carrizo Creek it turned north, crossing the mountains at Warner's Pass, and heading north to Los Angeles. From there it continued north over the San Bernadino Range and across the Sierra and central valley of California, and then west through Pacheco Pass to Gilroy and north to San Francisco.

On August 1, 1859, the Post Office Department changed the route from the Guadalupe Mountain passage to the extreme southern route via Forts Stockton, Davis, and Quitman, probably to give the posts the benefit of the mail service, but also partly to avail the coaches of the protection offered by the forts. This Davis Mountain route, which was known as the military road to El Paso, was safer from Indian attack and it followed the Rio Grande for 85 miles, thus assuring a water supply for that distance. It was, however, slightly longer. The change to the Davis Mountain route necessitated the establishment of a ferry at Horsehead Crossing, which was constructed in early August. From the crossing, the route went almost directly southwest to Fort Stockton, the first station on the new route, four miles away.

John Butterfield was given one year from the date of his contract to put the stage line in operation, and the problems that faced him in doing so were many and formidable. The energy and skill he applied to them was, however, typical of a man who had already made a reputation as one of the leading entrepreneurs in the coaching business in the country. Born at Berne, New York, November 18, 1801, Butterfield had little formal education. He became a stage driver at an early age, rose rapidly in the field, and soon was in control of several stage lines in New York.

At about the age of nineteen, Butterfield became a driver for the firm of Thorp and Sprague, of Albany, New York. In 1830 he moved to Utica, New York, to take a position as driver with another firm; there he also bought a horse and a two seat vehicle to start his own business "that soon rivaled the older established concerns at Utica." As an adjunct to his livery business he opened a boarding house, and after several years, in addition to his own thriving business, he assumed the management of the firm in which he had started as a driver, Parker and Company. He continued increasing his business "until he eventually held a controlling interest in most of the important mail and passenger coach lines in northern and western New York." He expanded in the packet-boat and steamer trade on Lake Ontario, and in 1849 he organized the Butterfield and Wasson Express Company, which he proposed to merge with two other already established lines, the Wells and Company, and the Livingston and Fargo. The merger resulted in the establishment of the American Express Company in 1850, of which he was a director until his death. Though not a politician, he was elected mayor of Utica in 1856.

When he received the government mail contract, Butterfield was fifty-six years old. Elected president of the Overland Mail Company, he immediately applied that same determination which had brought him success in his earlier endeavors to the organization of the new enterprise. The task facing him was nothing less than the construction of a road and the establishment of an efficient and regular running schedule over 2800 miles of terrain which was not only uninhabited for much of its expanse, but prohibitive in its ruggedness and lack of water. The land between Fort Smith and El Paso was "a thousand miles of wilderness, arid plains, deserts, and mountains, inhabited only by bands of roving Indians. The Marcy-Simpson Trail was a trail in name only, being no more than an indefinite route between rivers, springs, and water holes." Viewing these hindrances, Butterfield's opponents predicted he would never set up a line across the country and properly equip it. They underestimated the strength of the man's will and his ability.

As soon as the contract was signed, Butterfield set about putting it into effect. It was estimated that the original expenses involved in setting up the line came to about a million dollars. Not only the road itself had to be ready to receive the coaches, but animals, personnel, and equipment had to be purchased, distributed, and made ready for the opening of the service. Test runs had to be made and time schedules set up in advance of opening.

Butterfield began by making a survey of the entire route, "taking with him a staff composed of the most capable construction and operating superintendents of the four great express companies." He had previously sent out men to employ guides and scouts friendly to Indians and familiar with the territory the line would pass over. Maintaining good relations with the Indians on the route was always one of his chief concerns; after the line was in operation, he expended over $10,000 a year for the purchase of beef to distribute to them, and his men were under orders not to antagonize the Indians, even to the point of not attempting to shoot to kill when they raided the station to steal the company's stock. The company policy, however, generously permitted them to "shoot to kill" if their own lives or the mail itself were in danger. Just how strictly diligent the individual drivers and stationmasters were in adhering to this policy when the Indians started shooting may be doubtful, but, whether as a result of this policy or other circumstances, the Butterfield suffered less from Indian depredations than did other western stage lines—only ten of its drivers were killed.

The crews sent out on the survey were used to improve old roads over which the line would pass and to open new ones. They located favorable fords and ferrying places over rivers, located and constructed stations, and dug wells in places where water was otherwise unobtainable. One of the chief reasons for Butterfield's success when other operations failed was his appreciation of the necessity of establishing and maintaining good roads.

After the survey was completed, Butterfield divided the route into two sections, one east and one west of El Paso. Each was placed under the supervision of a general superintendent, and was further divided into nine subsections, with their own superintendents each of whom was responsibile for maintaining friendly relations with the Indians, hiring suitable employees, and constructing his own section of the line. After the line was put into operation he would make his headquarters at one of the way stations, supervise the relay posts on either side, and be held responsible for the maintenance of time schedules and the safety of passengers and

and mail on his division.

By September, 1858, when the mail was scheduled to go into operation, one hundred and forty-one stations were constructed and ready to operate, while by the first part of the next year nearly 200 were opened. In the summer of 1859 ten stations were abandoned on the Guadalupe Mountain route when it was changed to go by the Davis Mountains, where sixteen stations were added.

The stations were from eight to twenty-five miles apart, and at first some were even forty or fifty miles away, which meant that the coaches had to travel that distance without a change of teams. With the constant construction of new stations, the distance between them was continually reduced, until the distance between them averaged only ten or fifteen miles, except on the desert. The stations were of two types, "home stations," housing a station master, herders, harness makers, cooks, and blacksmiths, and "swing stations" where the teams were changed and only two or three men were maintained to perform this function. For the most part stations were new buildings, constructed especially for the line's use, but in a few instances old structures no longer used were converted for the purpose. Such were the old post buildings at Fort Phantom Hill.

Most of the stations were made of wood until the route entered New Mexico and Arizona, where they were more frequently made of the readily available adobe and constructed with large square enclosures for defense against the Indians. In a few instances where the Indian danger was particularly severe, stone was used in the building of the stations. They were built for utility, and comfort was not one of their strong points. The floors, according to one traveler, were "much like the ground outside, only not nearly so clean." Generally they were not constructed to accommodate the passengers who might travel on the coaches, ten minutes were expected to be the maximum time for a stop at most of them, with only a few providing accomodations for feeding passengers and keeping them for that purpose longer at the station.

To open operations the line purchased 100 coaches, 1000 horses, 500 mules, and recruited nearly 800 men, of whom 150 were drivers. The three major coach companies of the day supplied the Butterfield with coaches and wagons—The Abbot-Dowing Company, the James Good Company, and the Eaton, Gilbert Company. At first a regular "southern style" coach was used as far as Springfield, Missouri, where passengers transferred to spring wagons; later the coaches were used as far as Fort Smith.

The "southern style" coach carried nine inside passengers and theoretically an unlimited number of outside passengers. It was designed for the relatively smooth traveling conditions in the east, as well as perhaps for the impression it made on the public. It weighed 4,800 pounds, and was painted red or green, with designs and pictures painted on the lower panels of the doors. The interiors were furnished with russet leather lining, cushions, and side curtains, while wire pattern candle lamps hung outside to light the way. Its cost was $1,400 at the factory.

The "celerity" wagon, used on the rougher western sections of the route, was not at all designed for the impression it might make on passers-by; it was strictly utilitarian, and cost about $1,000. Lighter and faster than the Concord coach, it was also designed for rougher sections, with smaller wheels and a lower center of gravity; its carriage was similar to the regular coach; but it carried nine inside passengers only. It was designed as a sleeper for the long journey from Fort Smith to San Francisco, having three seats which made into a bed. The front seat faced backward while the middle seat was "often a removable stool-like arrangement with little or no support for the back." The body of the coach was white oak braced with iron bands suspended on two leather thoroughbraces extending the length of the coach. The thoroughbraces, three inches thick, were exceptionally rugged, as they served in place of springs over the rugged western terrain.

The teams pulling the coaches, usually horses until the desert and mountain country west of El Paso was entered, where mules were used, were made up of four animals, although in very mountainous or rugged country an additional brace was sometimes hitched. To provide for the animals, each station had to be provided with from fifty to one hundred tons of hay and grain each year, and sometimes with water as well, which might have to be hauled long distances to the station.

In the romantic legends that have grown up about the Butterfield mail, and in its own days as well, the man who guided the plunging teams across the prairies was the hero of the enterprise. His was the figure on which centered the adulation of the small boys who gathered to watch the stage come in, and the man around whom grew up stories of courage and skill in keeping the mail safe from hazards of Indians, thieves, and the harsh country beyond the Red River. But the driver was but one of many men who, though their daily role was less romantic, nevertheless insured the success of the Butterfield mail. The number of men employed at the stations numbered more than five hundred, only about a fourth of whom were drivers. The rest served in a number of capacities.

The wagons stopped at morning, noon, and evening for meals, and at those stations where they paused, cooks had to be provided. At stations especially liable to Indian attacks, four or five guards were stationed for defense. To inspect and treat the animals, veterinarians patrolled the routes; and at major stations blacksmiths, wheelwrights, and harness makers were maintained. And every station had a "keeper" who was accountable for the safety of the mail and passengers and for the conditions and protection of property and animals. His responsibilities extended so far that if the driver of the incoming stage were unable to continue, the keeper was required to take his place.

Each stage coach had a driver and a conductor, both of whom were armed when traveling in Indian territory. The driver, legend to the contrary, did not take the stage the entire length of the route, rather he was assigned a section of the line approximately sixty miles long. His driving was limited to this section, which he was expected to be familiar with, and he was to take the stages both ways between the stations at each end of his section. He was housed and fed at these end stations of his section. The conductor likewise had a section assigned to him, of approximately 120 miles. He had charge of the passengers and mail and was responsible for guarding them, until "he had received a detailed receipt from the next conductor." He was also bound to continue on beyond his own section if the next conductor was incapable of taking over. In addition to guarding the safety of the coach and its contents, the conductor notified the stations where teams would be changed of the arrival of his coach; for this purpose he used a brass bugle whose call to the men at the station could be heard from as far away as two miles. Occasionally men would be required for some special purpose, as when dangerous territory had to be crossed on an especially dark night, and a man had to ride ahead with a light to guide the way.

Letter mail and freight, in addition to passengers who might want to ride with it, were the only burdens carried on the Butterfield Mail. An exception was made in the case of a few leading newspapers from each coast which were carried as a courtesy and which for a long time provided the fastest means of obtaining news of the rest of the country. The line specifically refused to carry large amounts of money or valuables partly to discourage holdups and partly to divert that business to Wells Fargo, which was affiliated with the Overland. The cost of sending letters by way of the Overland Mail was ten cents per half ounce, and for freight it was $1.00 per 100 pounds per 100 miles.

For the person who chose to become a passenger on the Butterfield Overland Mail the fare was $100 from San Francisco east and $200 from St. Louis or Memphis west—the sums to be paid in gold. In January 1859 the eastern fare was raised to $200, but was lowered to $150 in May. This did not include meals, which could be purchased from 75 cents to $1.00, depending on the distance from a center of settlement of the particular station where the meal was taken; but forty pounds of baggage was allowed each passenger free of charge. Way passengers—those who were not traveling the entire route between St. Louis or Memphis and San Francisco were accommodated for the charge of fifteen cents per mile.

The first stages carrying mail for the Butterfield line left San Francisco and St. Louis on September 15, 1858, and both arrived ahead of schedule. This was to become a not uncommon occurrence; in spite of the skeptics who thought the line could never be a success, the majority of trips were made in from between twenty-one and twenty-three days, while twenty-five were allowed for the trip. Each Monday and Thursday coaches left Tipton and Santa Fe completing two trips weekly to each city. This was for the passenger service by coach; freight, which traveled by ox-wagon caravan, was much slower. Surprisingly, after the great debate that had raged for years over the necessity for the establishment of the overland mail, when the first coach actually departed, not only was there little enthusiasm, very little attention was even paid to it. According to William Ormsby who rode the first coach over the whole route and reported on his journey for the New York *Herald* he himself "was the only member of the press who witnessed the deposit of the first mail bag, en route for San Francisco overland, in the cars of the Pacific Railroad Company, at St. Louis," and "only about a dozen letters and a few papers were entrusted to its care." The local newspapers evidently considered the event of no consequence, for their columns ignored it. Said Ormsby, when the coach left Tipton, Missouri, "not a cheer was raised as the coach . . . set out."

But J. M. Farwell, who wrote of the trip east for the *Daily Alta California*, found the reception of his coach in St. Louis somewhat different. "Cheering crowds led by the St. Louis Silver Band escorted driver and passengers to the Planters Hotel; once more, toasts were drunk to the success of John Butterfield and his bridging of the continent. From Washington the President of the United States wired: "I cordially congratulate you upon the result. It is a glorious triumph for civilization and the Union."

In spite of skepticisms and apathy alike, the Overland Mail during its two and a half years of existence, provided surprisingly reliable service. Not all of its sections were uniformly efficient; the Memphis branch was far below that from St. Louis in the quality of its service; but on the whole the accomplishments of the line were exceptional.

The obstacles to successful operation of the mail service were many. Indians, which are generally what first occurs to those who try to recall what a trip on the stage must have been like, were, curiously, one of the least of the line's worries. There is only one report of an open attack on the mail coach as it was en route; this occured at Apache Pass, Arizona, in 1861, and was not intended as an assault on the line itself, but was peripheral to a battle the Apaches were then engaged upon with the U.S. Army. In the first year of the company's operations, the Indians were content to make off with the stock of the company; later, when the company began using mules instead of horses in those regions heavily frequented by Indians, they began to demand supplies instead. Under strict instructions, the station keepers were as likely to provide the supplies as to encourage attack by refusing them; more than any other stage line, the Butterfield maintained good relationship with the Indians; where possible it manned stations in Indian territories with men who were conversant in the Indians' own languages and who were adept at dealing with them.

Far more frequent threats to the running of the mails than attacks by Indians were less dramatic incidents, but ones which occurred with much more regularity. The danger of the stages overturning, with loss of life or at the very least such damage to the coach that the mail was held up, was always present. Considering the nature of the country the stages traversed, this was an infrequent occurrence, but it did occur; in one such accident near Fort Smith, a stage overturned, killing one passenger immediately, and seriously injuring several others. At times too, equipment was unavailable when needed, so that coaches were forced to borrow, from army encampments on their routes arms and ammunition, and even replacements for their jaded mules.

But the most frequent difficulty experienced by the coaches as they crossed the country was the problem of keeping trained animals for the teams, and of keeping the coaches running when such teams were not available. When the Indians made off with the relays for incoming teams, station keepers were forced to seize what wild animals they could find and hitch them to the stages. That the stages moved at all under the circumstances is something of a wonder. As one rider on the coaches wrote, "Nothing but the most perfect presence of mind on the part of the driver could prevent accidents. Even this was not always enough, as was proved by a stage which we met, in which every passenger had either a bandaged head or an arm in a sling." The writer later experienced some of the same himself. "Today, on having a relay of mustangs, they reared up and plunged worse than usual, broke the pole-chain, stood up nearly perpendicularly, and, finally, one fell and got underneath the body of the wagon, which movement, together with the threatening kicks and jerks of the animals, caused our speedy evacuation of the vehicle, till order was restored and the journey resumed."

Ormsby described the process of attempting to turn one of the wild beasts into a docile draft animal:

> First he had to be secured with a laretto round his neck, and drawn by main force to a tree or post; then the harness had to be put on piece by piece, care being taken to avoid his teeth and heels. Althogether, I should estimate the time consumed in the process at not less than half an hour to each wild mule, and that, when the mail has to wait for it, might, I think, much better be spent on the road.

After the team was hitched to the coach, the procedure was to tear off the blindfolds, leap back from the flying hooves, and allow them to run away over the prairie, no attempt to guide them being made until their first energies were spent and they became somewhat more docile. Before that point was reached, however, they "reared, pitched, twisted, whirled, wheeled, ran, stood still, and cut up all sorts of capers." The theory was that they would become gradually accustomed to working in harness, after which they could be easily guided. It was a sort of "on the job training" for the teams, and until they had completed the course, the driver did very well indeed merely to keep them somewhere near the road.

The best picture of what the passage of the overland mail from one half of the continent to the other was like comes from the journals kept by passengers who made the trip. Most of them marked the discomforts and dangers of the trip, but seemed quickly to become accustomed to them; as one of them noted, almost all the riders said they were unable to sleep the first week for the tremendous bouncing and jolting and the hard seats, but after the initiation period, they ceased to notice it. Ormsby wrote that the dangers and hardships of the trip were not so bad as he expected; there were no Indian attacks, and the staked plain, which he had expected to be the worst part of the trip, was not difficult because the wagon carried its own water supply. He arrived in San Francisco, "safe and sound from all the threatened dangers of Indians, tropic suns, rattlesnakes, grizzly bears, stubborn mules, mustang horses, jerked beef, terrific mountain passes, fording rivers, and all the concomitants which envy, pedantry, and ignorance had predicted for all passengers by the overland mail routes over which I have just passed. . . ." During his trip, he had even begun to "get quite enthusiastic on the subject of the mail myself, and looked upon the mail bags and the horses with quite as much interest as I should have had in the Atlantic cable had I been on that world renowned expedition. I jumped out and got water for the horses, kept an eye on the mail bags, walked up the steep hills, and forgot the terrible pain in the back which such incessant riding without sleep occasioned."

Meals were something on which all passengers remarked. Ormsby noted that "the fare, though rough, is better than could be expected so far from civilized districts, and consists of bread, tea, and fried steaks of bacon, venison, antelope, or mule flesh—the latter tough enough. Milk, butter, and vegetables can only be met with towards the two ends of the route—that is, in California and at the "stations" in the settled parts of the western Mississippi Valley." Fried in a grease-encrusted and blackened skillet, whose wielder seldom recognized the virtues of soap and water, the main course was seldom sufficient to whet the appetite of even the famished travelers. Famous on the route was the probably apocryphal tale of the stationmaster who placed before a traveler the entree of fat pork. "Thank you," said the guest, "but I never I never eat it." "Very well," replied his host, "just help yourself to the mustard." Fastidious palates received no gratification on the Overland Stage. The usual beverage was "lethally black" coffee, but there were occasional alternatives. Mark Twain, travelling some years later on the successor to the Butterfield, told of a peculiar speciality of the stationmaster, "a beverage which he called "Slumbullion," and it is hard to think he was not inspired when he named it. It really pretended to be tea, but there was too much dish-rag, and sand, and old bacon-rind in it to deceive the intelligent traveller."

Many travellers, like Ormsby, were at first impressed by the strange forms of plants and animals to be observed in the west; but like him they often pronounced, after long monotonous miles, the whole journey a bore.

They could not resist, however, adding to the character of what they did observe when they journalized their adventures. William Tallack, who made the trip in 1860 was particularly colorful in describing the wildlife he saw. Of the tarantula he wrote, "Its eyes are prominent and glisten with mischief and evil." But his best description is of the "dogtowns," or burrows of the "prairie marmot" as he called the prairie dog.

> Amongst them are numerous rattlesnakes and small owls, both of which appear in good condition, and are popularly said to form a vast "happy family" with the marmots; but the probability is (considering the usual relations which subsist between snakes, owls, and small weak quadrupeds) that the "happiness" of such communities is very one-sided, and that the little prairie dogs and their young not only afford lodgings to their feathered and scaly neighbors by their burrowing labours, but board also, at the expense of their own sleek and rounded bodies.

In April of 1860, John Butterfield resigned as president of the company because of a physical breakdown. But by this time it had been demonstrated that the mail could succeed, and he had selected his subordinates so well that the mail continued to run as before until outside influences brought it to a close.

There had been a tremendous increase in the amount of mail carried over the route since its inception; in December, 1859, only 1143 letters were carried in a single trip, but in July of the next year a mail of 6020 letters left San Francisco. Not until 1860 did the number of letters transported overland exceed those carried by ship; in November 1859, the average number of letters carried by stage was 5000, while 25,000 went by steamer. But in 1860 the Butterfield line surpassed the ships.

Passenger traffic, on the other hand, never lived up to the expectations of the line. It was never heavy, but usually every coach carried some passengers. Many of them evidently found the continuous riding day and night intolerable, for it became customary for them to interrupt their trips to remain at intermediate stations to rest. This undoubtedly put something of a strain on the resources of the line, for most of the stations had not been constructed to provide for the accommodation of guests. During the first year of operation, the number of through passengers was only about one hundred and fifty each way. Frequently there were no through passengers from the east, and the number did not generally exceed two. During the life of the line, the number of through passengers increased.

In 1858-59 there was much talk in Congress of reforming the Post Office Department and cutting its large deficit. In the latter year Post Master Brown died, and was replaced by Joseph Holt, who viewed his new domain as a self-supporting business and one to be conducted on a business basis. By abandoning some lines, and cutting the service of others, Holt reduced the annual expenditure of postal service to the Pacific coast from $2,184,697, to $908,687. This was still not enough to compensate for the deficit accumulated on these lines, for their receipts were only $339,747.34. Holt's views on the Post Office Department were explicit:

> The transportation and delivery of the mail with the utmost dispatch and security are the true and only mission of this department; in accomplishing this, it discharges its whole duty to the country.... There are those who maintain that the adjustment of the mail service should be made subservient, if not subordinate to the interest of commerce and travel, and that the rapid and cheap conveyance of passengers and the support of railroad, steamship and stage companies, should as carefully be looked to and as anxiously provided for by the department as the transportation of the mails. This is a fatal fallacy whose bitter fruits may now be seen in the enormous sums paid to these companies for mails, some of which are so light as scarcely to yield a revenue sufficient to defray the expense of carrying them on horseback. Four horse coaches are thus run upon border and unfrequented routes, and steamboat lines are subsidized at an outlay which would afford postal accommodations to entire states.

With this attitude it was natural that Holt should wish to make changes in the Butterfield route, which was both long and duplicative of the Birch routes from San Antonio. But the terms of the Butterfield contract did not permit this, so it was not until the impending of the Civil War threatened to stop the service entirely that he was able to do so. By 1860, however, the best days of the Butterfield Overland Company were passing as the spectre of the Civil War loomed on the horizon. Already the government was anticipating the fate of the southern route and was closing and modifying sections of mail routes in the southwest.

On March 5, 1861, Texas withdrew from the Union, and the fate of the Butterfield was sealed. It attempted to continue operations, but now it was no longer the great service uniting the two sections of a single nation, but an intruder from the land of the Yankees. Now it was considered open game for Confederate hotheads, and the stations in Texas territory soon became victims of citizens who "seized the supplies of the company at certain stations, and seem to have taken some of the stock and coaches," though the "official policy of the state government seems to have been to leave the company alone until it should become necessary to stop all communications between the North and South...." When it became obvious that Texas was not safe territory for the coaches, the company attempted to maintain an irregular schedule as far as Fort Smith from the east and Tucson from San Francisco, but this resulted in a huge backlog of accumulated mail The last mail to the east was therefore made up at Tucson where there was the largest accumulation; it left on March 6. The last mail from the east left for San Francisco in the early part of April, 1861; with these trips ended the history of the Butterfield Overland Company on the southern route through Texas.

The experience of the last coach passing through Texas was typical of the new attitude toward the mail line on the part of the south. Approaching Fort Chadbourne, the stage was overtaken by a party of Texas troops. The driver and passengers "sat on nervous seats" as the Texans parted to allow them passage. Then the driver invoked what had been the signal for the cheers of admiring crowds, "carrying the United States Mail." The rebels laughed in his face, and leapt off their horses to seize his wheels, " and shouted at him to drive on." But, as a passenger later reported, he "could not, with the greatest whipping, induce the horses to proceed." At last the pranksters wearied of their sport and permitted the coach to proceed, but not before they had amply demonstrated their contempt for the mail of the United States government.

Offically the Butterfield Overland Mail service from St. Louis to San Francisco had ended on March 2, 1861, when Congress authorized the Post Master General to discontinue the southern route and made a new contract to run over the central route. The new service was to provide daily mail service from St. Joseph, Missouri, or Atchison, Kansas, to Placerville, and Sacramento, California, as well as Denver and Salt Lake City, including a letter mail to San Francisco. It was also to run a pony express semi-weekly eight months of the year on a ten day schedule, and for four months of the year on a twelve day schedule. The pony express was to operate until the completion of the overland telegraph. Compensation for the entire operation was to be $1,000,000 per year.

Following the closure of the Butterfield Mail, an unsuccessful attempt was made to restore service on the southern route. In May, 1861, a contract was made with G. H. Giddings for the Overland Mail Line to carry the mail from San Antonio to California. The Overland Mail Line was the successor to the old San Antonio and San Diego Mail Line; as the Overland it was to maintain a service between Los Angeles and Monterey, with its main line from San Antonio to Fort Stockton and an extension via Tucson to Los Angeles. The company, however, could not fulfill the terms of its contract, chiefly because of the turmoil brought on by the Civil War, and its contract was cancelled in July of 1861.

On the central route, the Butterfield company adopted a different method of conducting the business from what it had maintained on the southern route; instead of operating the entire route itself, it subcontracted all but a 550 mile section between Salt Lake City and Virginia City. The eastern section to Salt Lake City and the Denver cut off route were leased to the Central Overland California and Pike's Peak Express Company, while the western section from Virginia City to

Sacramento was leased to the Pioneer Stage Company. For a period of three months, while it was involved in making the change from its southern route, the Butterfield did not furnish service. But on July 1, 1861, the first mail left St. Joseph, and on July 18, it reached San Francisco.

The movement to the central route was the beginning of the decline of the Butterfield mail; its operations were not nearly so efficient as they had been on the southern route, and were a source of much criticism. Because of winter snow, ice, and mud, it could only operate successfully eight months of the year. An attempt to combat this was made by shifting the route from the North Platte to the South Platte via Julesburg, with Atchison, Kansas, as the eastern terminus; in 1867 when the Butterfield company no longer operated the line, it was moved further south to Smokey Hill river route by way of Fort Riley, with Leavenworth as the eastern terminus. Indians, too, gave more trouble to the line than they had on the southern route. For a time they so disrupted the regularity of service that the bulk of letter mail was shifted once again to ocean service. And, with the coming of the Civil War, fares began to increase; the charge for passenger service from Atchison or St. Joseph to Placerville was $200, and from Placerville to San Francisco $10.00 with only a twenty-five pound baggage allowance. Meals were extra, as they had been on the southern route, but their cost was now from $1.00 to $1.50.

The Pony Express service of the Butterfield's central route was intended to run between the terminus of the transcontinental telegraph line then being constructed, and to end when the telegraph was completed. Modeled after the original Pony Express founded by William H. Russell, it also began operating in July, 1861, running between Ft. Kearney, and Placerville, and was discontinued October 24, 1861, when the Overland Telegraph line was completed.

In 1862 the Central Overland Company found itself unable to meet its financial obligations, and on March 21, it transferred its contract with the consent of the Post Office Department, to Ben Holladay. Holladay had made a distinguished name for himself in the history of the overland stage companies, but his entrance upon the scene marked the end of the life of the Butterfield. The contract under which the Overland Mail had operated expired on June 30, 1864, but as there was no successor ready to start operating on July 1, it continued service to Placerville to September 30. The Post Office Department, meanwhile, advertised for bids on a new contract. The route was divided into two sections, an eastern division from Atchison to Salt Lake City, including Denver service, and a western division from Salt Lake City to Folsom City. On August 19, 1864, contracts were awarded to Holladay at $365,000 per year for the eastern section, and to William B. Dinsmore for $385,000 for the western section. Both contracts provided for daily service to last to September 30, 1868. In November, 1866, both Holladay's and Dinsmore's contracts were taken over by Wells Fargo and Company.

On September 30, 1868, when this contract expired, the Post Office Department awarded a new contract, on the basis of the lowest bid, to Carlton Spaids of Chicago for $335,000, even though the Wells Fargo Company was the only one in existence with sufficient experience and equipment to operate the service. Spaid failed to begin the service, and apparently made little effort to put it into operation; by the middle of October all mail was halted between Mississippi and the Pacific and a huge backlog had accumulated. Driven by necessity, the Post Office Department made a new contract with Wells Fargo to carry the mail "between the terminals of the Pacific railroads at a rate of $1,750,000 per annum subject to a pro rata for every section of fifty miles of railroad completed." The joining of the east and west rails of the Union Pacific at Promontory Point, Utah, on May 10, 1869, automatically cancelled the Wells Fargo contract. So ended the overland transcontinental mail service that had begun eleven years before under the aegis of the Butterfield Mail Company.

The three years of its operation in the southwest had not been wasted; though the accomplishments of its brief career were perhaps more spectacular than substantial, its influence would endure long after it had passed from the scene. It was the foremost institution in the development and expansion of the area in which it operated. During the period of its existence the population of the chief towns along its routes nearly doubled, and numerous smaller settlements, each with its post office, sprung up along its path.

> For a quarter of a century after its abandonment, the Butterfield trail continued to be the main artery of traffic in the southwest for the emigrant, the trader, and the drover. It became the military road between Texas and California, and the route followed by all the various sets of mail contractors up to the time of the forming of the railroad. To all these, the wells sunk and tanks built by the old organization, provided the only available water through the desert region, and the deserted mail stations and corrals furnished shelter, storage facilities, and often times protection from the Indians. The railroad builders coming after also profited by the labors of those early road builders, and established their grades in many places in the very ruts of the old trail. . .

While the great Concord coaches of the Butterfield line rolled over the southern route, no area felt their influence more than did the Lone Star State. The population of the counties through which the coaches traveled increased rapidly between 1858 and 1860, particularly in Grayson, Denton, Wise, Jack, and Young counties. And not only the numbers of the people, but their attitudes as well, were influenced by the access to news from the east provided by the coaches. After 1858, the papers of Texas show an increasingly staunch stand being taken for the southern states in the disputes with the north. And the mail company brought not only people to Texas, but in some measure business as well. Frequently the line's stations became the center of the business district, as in El Paso, where the station was the largest and best equipped of the company-built stations on the route. The great supply line required to maintain the line's operations became a source of income for numbers of men not directly engaged by the company.

To the people of its own day, Butterfield mail provided a continuing link with the friends and relatives left at home when they departed for the west, and a source of news about what was happening in the more populated areas of the nation. It lessened the sense of isolation which had dominated large sections of the west, and in Texas in particular served to draw the state away from its sense of an independent and unique history, and to push it into union with what would soon be the Confederate States of America. The Butterfield was a part of the frontier expansionism that had dominated the country since the 1840's and was one of the agents that helped to conquer the west. Ormsby had predicted that "one of the greatest benefits of the establishment of this overland mail route will be that it will indicate to the immigrant, with his valuable droves of cattle, the safest and surest means of transit across these waterless plains. . . ." It showed the way to a generation of immigrants and it would show the way later for the railroads, not only in tracing a physical route, but in reassuring America that the west was within its grasp. To generations who came after it, the Butterfield overland mail would symbolize the spirit that made the west, in character as in fact, a part of the United States. The instructions of old John Butterfield, to the men who guided his coaches across the wilderness might equally be applied to the settlers whose lumbering wagons followed the trail of the racing mail wagons: "Remember, boys, nothing on God's earth must stop the United States mail."

The Old San Antonio Road
by **JOE B. FRANTZ**

Illustrations by:
Melvin C. Warren

Melvin C. Warren — 1968

HODDING CARTER called it the *Doomed Road of Empire,* with a subtitle of *The Spanish Trail of Conquest.* Many people call it simply *The Old San Antonio Trail,* or *The Old San Antonio Road,* or *The Spanish Trail.* The varieties of name are of interest only to those persons entranced with detail. It was definitely El Camino Real, The Royal Road of the Spanish from Northern Mexico across Texas into Louisiana.

Like an historic trail, the Old San Antonio Road's precise route is argued by the purists. Such arguments are of no concern here. In brief, it began at the provincial capital of Saltillo, came down across the *polvo* of Coahuila through the sometime provincial capital of Monclova, crossed the Rio Grande del Norte between Laredo and Del Rio, continued through the huisache and catclaw into San Antonio de Bexar, through the increasingly more luxuriant German country of later New Braunfels, below Austin and beside Bastrop, north of a future settlement of considerable historic but little commercial concern, Washington-on-the-Brazos, through Crockett, Nacogdoches, San Augustine, past the future Gaines' Ferry, and finally into Natchitoches, sometimes Spanish, sometimes French. It was a long road designed to cement and protect an empire that was hopelessly strung out and generally empty. It covered a thousand miles from the complete aridity beyond Saltillo to the mildew and moss of Louisiana.

Originally, of course, the country all belonged to one or another group of Indians. However, those Indians along the trail were generally not the type that excited Spanish greed, and therefore Spanish interest. They told no tales of vast golden wealth several moons away, nor did they tend to sit still long enough to develop the sort of culture the Spanish might exploit. One reason for building the trail, of course, was to insure mission contact, but as religious efforts the missions enjoyed minimum success.

Because of the generally nomadic culture of the Indians along the trail and because the trail itself gave so little promise for a sedentary culture, the Spanish made only intermittent attempts to colonize the Indians. They did gather tribes around the missions, they taught them a little bit about farming, they deplored them as they ran off at the first sign of spring, and they welcomed them back with some cynicism when these natural children ran out of food and concomitantly their desire for the wild, free, but hungry life.

Two tribes that the Spanish had little early contact with were the Apaches and the Comanches. However, once these two groups learned from the Spanish to utilize the horse and to make their own saddles, they pushed against everything which got in their way. The Spanish being athwart their path, the Indians menaced the newcomers and formed a considerable and effective barrier to Spanish expansion in Texas.

In general, the Spanish behaved just like the Anglo-Saxons who were moving westward from their Atlantic bases. They simply destroyed the Indians, either by killing them or by weakening their culture until, in effect, the Indians destroyed themselves. Disease was introduced. Other Indians were run off to survive somewhere else. The Karankawas hated the Spanish, while as time went by the Tonkawas turned toward the Anglo-Americans in opposition to the Spanish. If the Spanish didn't destroy the Indians, then other Indians, notably Comanches, made their own inroads on other tribes along El Camino Real. The proud Indian heritage that adds so richly to the *sabor* of Mexican life today simply never existed in Texas, nor did the Spanish absorb and overlay the little Indian cultures in Texas as adroitly as they did with the major cultures which they found in Mexico's central valley.

Actually, the Old Spanish Trail is often said to have begun with the coming of the French into Texas and Spanish determination to keep their European neighbor out of this part of the New World. Conception of the road precedes La Salle's disaster, although the admixture of French dreams, Gallic misery, and a bloody *denouement* undoubtedly intensified Spanish desires to get a proper highway established. Origin of the trail dates from the coming of the Spanish into the little patch of greenness soon to be named Saltillo. Twenty families moved into the valley in 1575, under the illusion that it was a "high land of many waters." There were numerous springs, but the limits to which the water could be channeled were restricted. Nonetheless men grew crops around Saltillo, which has the advantage of possessing the last equable climate before descending into the hot lands that stretch from present-day Monterrey and Monclova all the way across the inhospitable half of Texas. Although no one knew it in the 1580's, Saltillo is the last oasis from the moment one moves down the almost limitless valley to its north until the burned-out traveler finally winds up in San Antonio.

Over the next three-quarters of a century other settlements were made for a hundred leagues or more to the northward of Saltillo. Miserable and undistinguished, they were nonetheless important as road signs to the future. By 1682 the *camino real* had stretched from Saltillo almost to the Rio Grande del Norte. How long it would have taken to have made a real trail out of this slow progress under ordinary circumstances can only be conjectured, but extraordinary circumstances shortly prevailed.

In France, René Robert Cavelier Sieur de La Salle, that intrepid aristocrat who first traveled the Mississippi from Illinois to its mouth, was ready for a bolder stroke. Having established New France in some vague Louisiana, he needed to back up his claim with new effort. The result was that he persuaded his King, his friends, and even himself to invest in four ships to start on a secret colonizing mission in the New World. They sailed out with the usual gaiety, reached Hispañola, and learned about pirates and hurricanes. They also learned that the climate in the Caribbean can debilitate. By this time they were down to three ships.

Nevertheless they sailed once again, ran into calms and fogs, and finally reached a shore. They had missed the Mississippi, the evident point for their colonization, and instead had hit what today is called Matagorda in Texas. They named the area St. Louis, for reasons that are only too obvious. Realizing that he had selected a place unsuitable for landing, La Salle marched down the coast for a better anchorage, choosing the mouth of the Lavaca River. His headquarters ship, *L'Aimable*, promptly wrecked on the shoals at Pass Caballo; with the ship went its valuable cargo. A second ship, the *Belle*, made several trips into the area before being wrecked about March 1, 1685. Meanwhile the third ship, the *Joli*, had returned to France.

Ashore then was a group of glorious Gauls, already dissident. Nonetheless they built their Fort St. Louis, finishing by mid-summer 1685. La Salle made expeditions from the fort, apparently seeking both assistance and knowledge. Finding Indians who did not like the Spanish, he was encouraged about his possibilities of driving the Spanish from the land. Whatever a man wishes to think, he can usually find evidence to convince him in that direction. La Salle was as full of self-delusion as any ordinary man.

Next he went looking for the Mississippi River, knowing that without assistance either from home or from another French colony his future was poor. He passed the Colorado and Brazos rivers, moved through the Hasinai Indian country along the Trinity and Neches rivers, and caught fever. By the time he and his teen-age nephew had recovered, their ammunition was so low and their party so disspirited that they decided to return to Fort St. Louis. Twenty men had begun the journey; only eight returned. Desertion, inability to travel, and even the mouth of an alligator accounted for the losses.

Really the trip broke up over a buffalo bone, or rather, its marrow. A party of Frenchmen, including the surgeon Liotót, went looking for buffalo. When they did not return as expected, others went searching. One of the Frenchmen, Moranget, violated protocol by eating the marrow from Liotót's bone. The men argued. The other hungry men ranged to either side. All day long the argument continued. That night, after everyone was asleep, Liotót, like Lizzie Borden, took an axe, and gave "many strokes" to Sieur Moranget. The surgeon moved on, killing two others.

In camp, La Salle wondered where both the hunting party and the searching party had strayed. He too went looking. As he approached a river bank, he could see buzzards overhead. Coming upon a bloody cravat belonging to one of his men, he fired his musket to indicate that he was near. This unfortunate shot set up his ambush, as he fell on March 20, 1687, his body abandoned in the brush for the ants and the animals. Thus the end of real leadership for the French threat in Texas.

But the Spanish, of course, did not know how disastrous and disorganized an expedition the French had mounted nor how murderous some of the purported colonists had become. All they knew was that the French had landed and that the cause of Nueva España was threatened. If they were not to be forced out, they must get on with their organization.

The result was the appointment of Domingo Terán de los Rios as a road builder for Texas. Governor Terán was the first official governor for the Province of the Tejas and adjacent regions, beginning in 1691. He brought a reputation of long Spanish service in Peru and as a governor of Sonora and Sinaloa, where he was particularly noted as an Indian fighter. His commission instructed him to establish missions among the Tejas Indians, to learn the depth of French penetration, and to prepare a prospectus on Texas. It was Terán's group which named most of the Texas rivers between the Rio Bravo and the Sabine. Terán himself explored all the way to the Caddo settlements on the Red River before the end of 1691. In East Texas, where he found little to cheer him, he probably is responsible for the abandonment of the missions in that region.

More specifically, Terán in 1691 marked a trail from Monclova, enjoying one of its periods as provincial capital, all the way across Texas. It is the same road that St. Denis was to follow a quarter of a century later, and again the same trail which Moses Austin moved down when he went to get his grant of land that marks the real coming of the Anglo-American into Texas.

Associated with Governor Terán, to the pleasure of neither, was Fray Damián Manzanet, a Majorcan priest and confessor who had visited Texas in 1680 with Alonso de León in an effort to discover the location of La Salle's colony. Father Manzanet was given charge of the missionary work in Texas, and it was because of his formal report to the viceroy in September, 1690, that the Terán expedition was founded. Father Manzanet wanted a Spanish settlement along the Rio Guadalupe, plus seven missions. He received his seven missions, but not his Guadalupe village.

On the Terán expedition Father Manzanet was invariably annoyed because Terán did not seem to get on with his explorations with sufficient celerity. Thus, when it was time for Terán to return to Mexico, the charitable Christian father refused to lend him horses for the journey.

Manzanet seemed to have gotten along with the Indians about as well as he had gotten along with Governor Teran. When flood and disease hurt his missionary work, Indian resentment rose until the good father decided that a presidio was even more necessary than a simple evangelizing effort. When no one listened, he burned the mission of San Francisco, where he was stationed, and set out for Coahuila. Although the party became lost for nearly a month and a half in country that is difficult enough when one knows where he is, his group finally reached Monclova in mid-February, 1694. Although the viceroy asked Manzanet for assistance in upgrading the mission effort, the father had seen enough of Texas. He retired to the quiet collegiate life of Querétaro.

The next traveler of note along the Old Spanish Trail is another Frenchman, Louis Juchereau de St. Denis, out of Quebec and Louisiana. He had accompanied Bienville on an exploration up the Red River and had also commanded a fort below New Orleans. In 1713 the French governor of Louisiana, with the saleable name (by 1968 standards) of Cadillac, asked St. Denis to put the *camino real* to true commercial use. Accordingly, St. Denis left the Indian village at Natchitoches and struck out for San Juan Bautista on the Rio Grande, arriving there in mid-July 1714. With the store of attractiveness of any good Frenchman he made friends at San Juan, including the seventeen-year-old granddaughter of Diego Ramón, the commandant. So thirty-nine-year-old St. Denis wooed seventeen-year-old Manuela Sánchez. Stories of the success of the courtship vary, but for jealousy or other reasons St. Denis seems to have been in great danger of being removed to Mexico City under arrest. The orders may have come from no less than the viceroy himself.

Certainly St. Denis wound up in Mexico City, where he was seen by some old French friends now serving Spain. They persuaded the viceroy to let St. Denis stay with a Spanish officer outside the prison. There the viceroy himself met him, liked him, and wound up asking him to dinner. Soon the viceroy was planning with St. Denis a colonizing expedition back into Texas that would create first one, then four, and finally six new missions. Not only that, but he gave his recent prisoner a wedding present of 1,000 pesos, a fine bay horse, and a military escort to Manuela. The man who had been sent to Mexico to be placed in chains had wound up as the grandson-in-law of the commandant and a friend of His Excellency the Viceroy, the Duke de Linares. Small wonder that his wedding celebration lasted three days amid joy and wine without stint.

Diego Ramón had a son named Domingo, an uncle of Manuela. It was decided that Domingo Ramón should lead an expedition into Texas to see whether there were other Frenchmen like St. Denis lurking about to steal unwary granddaughters. Along the way they would reoccupy East Texas and resuscitate the mission effort. To the surprise of everyone, or perhaps of no one, St. Denis went along. Northeasterly across Texas the expedition progressed, loaded partially with the gear of war and partially with the ornaments of spirituality. It was quite an expedition, with a thousand goats, a thousand horses and sheep, and a host of provisions and agricultural and artisan supplies. The Franciscans were as imposing as the soldiers. Altogether an estimated 65 to 78 persons made the trip. They crossed the Rio Grande on April 20, 1716, and reached East Texas two months later. Along the way they established six missions and a presidio. They remained in East Texas until one of the new missions, San Miguel, was captured by the French, which caused the entire Spanish expedition to withdraw in 1719. The capture also proved what the Spanish had feared, that the French were not to be trusted and were in Texas in force.

St. Denis, incidentally, extended his personal *camino real* on to Mobile, where he carried articles brought from Mexico, in defiance of prohibitions of trade between the French and Mexican provinces. But the man was a confirmed smuggler, as well as an inveterate optimist and believer in his own luck. He returned to the Rio Grande in the spring of 1717, only to have his goods confiscated and to be himself transported to Mexico City to languish in a jail from June until the end of November on a charge of engaging in contraband. Out on bond, he escaped to Natchitoches, brought Manuela to join him, and set up a trading post for the remainder of his life. He irritated the Spanish officials considerably by consistently trading with their people in defiance of embargoes for more than a score of years. But he had shown that with a little nerve and imagination the *camino real* could indeed be a royal road to personal riches, despite the absence of mineral wealth.

About this time a new mission was added to the Texas scene and to the *camino real,* one that has occupied an emotional niche in the

Texas hall of remembrances ever since. When Father Manzanet and Governor Terán had come along the Old San Antonio Trail in 1691, they had stopped at an Indian village known as Yanaguana. Since the day of the visit was St. Anthony's Day—June 13—each man wrote in his diary, "I named it San Antonio de Padua." The soldier had recommended the site for a pueblo, while the priest had suggested it would be ideal for a mission. However, it required nearly a third of a century before either dream was realized. Men came and men went, both military and clerical, and usually sent back recommendations for something more nearly permanent. But nothing happened. Then in 1718 Father Antonio Olivares and Governor Martín de Alarcón, at odds with each other, converged on the area to carry out the recommendations of nearly three decades before. The result was the founding of the Villa de Bexár, named after the brother of the viceroy, and of the mission, San Antonio de Valero.

The mission quickly ran into the type of trouble which was going to stay with it until the twentieth century. A hurricane destroyed part of it, again in 1774 the major chapel collapsed, and altogether it endured five locations before it was finally settled. At the time that it became a Texas shrine it had once again been virtually abandoned and was crumbling. Following the famous siege of the Alamo, Texas permitted the mission to continue its disintegration until at the beginning of the twentieth century a determined group of patriotic women decided to resurrect it on a permanent basis before it was completely obliterated and replaced by commercial establishments. These women, the Daughters of the Republic of Texas, are as much heroines of the Alamo as the men on both sides who gave their lives there are its heroes. Without them, the Alamo would have become a plaque marking a site where something once happened, without any tangible recollection of the death and Texas transfiguration that occurred there.

Meanwhile San Antonio was developing into the major city along the *camino real*. Considering the competition, this statement does not exactly exalt the town. But the Canary Islanders had come in, bringing a flavor to the city which persists to this day. Others, attracted by the pleasant location, drifted in until San Antonio was designated a provincial sub-capital. And when Spain acquired Louisiana, it evacuated the missions in East Texas. Since they never had been too successful either as missions or forts, Spain decided it could live without them. This left San Antonio and the Alamo as gathering places for the dispossessed. In 1794 the Alamo was secularized. Shortly afterwards, the Alamo became a barracks, a foreboding of its destiny 33 years later. It also served briefly as a military hospital after 1806. In fact, its program of vaccination, free to those unable to pay, helped stop a smallpox epidemic.

In 1813 San Antonio and the Alamo were taken over by their first group of Anglo-Americans under Augustus Magee, who had been convinced by Bernardo Gutierrez that Texas could be made independent of Mexico. It was all part of a grand follow-up to Father Hidalgo's thrust for Mexican independence of

Spain. But the North Americans showed an inability to get along with themselves, reducing their efficiency, and before long the Spanish were back in control of the town and the mission-fort. The Spanish, however, felt that a real threat had taken place, and for that matter, the future Mexicans were also alarmed at how easily the Anglo-Americans had moved in. Once they were free of Spanish domination, many of the independent Mexicans would wonder whether it was possible to share the land with the *yanquis.*

After the Alamo had been recaptured, the Spanish turned it into a sort of prison for those San Antonians who had seemed friendly. Altogether 800 prisoners were rounded up, of whom the battle captives represented only a comparative handful. Most of the executions which followed took place away from the Alamo at the Military Plaza. The worst execution period of all occurred when 300 citizens were staked into an airless granary one night. Many suffocated, and those who survived were executed the next morning. To many it seemed as if the whole summer was one of legal murder.

Meanwhile along other parts of the trail, Texas was heading toward a feeling for separate entity. Along the eastern border, Athanese de Méziéres had survived the change-over of Louisiana from French to Spanish. De Méziéres, a son-in-law of St. Denis, had been so highly recommended to the Spanish that in November 1769 they had named him the lieutenant-governor at Natchitoches and four years later promoted him to lieutenant colonel. His job was to win for the Spanish from the Indian tribes of northern Texas the allegiance which had formerly belonged to the French. De Méziéres summoned the Indian chiefs to Natchitoches, established trading rules, and ran off the unfriendly. He made five trips over nine years throughout northern Texas and all the way to San Antonio, recording accounts of the trips in reports that have attracted attention from scholars of frontier statecraft ever since. It is no surprise that in 1778 he was made acting governor of Texas and in the next year, just before his death, he was appointed governor. He had as much to do with settling the Indian affairs in eastern Texas as any man in this state's long history. The fact is that unlike so much of the country to the West, when East Texas began to fill with white population it suffered very little Indian-white warfare. One reason for the orderly intrusion of Anglo-Americans into this part of the Indian world was the careful ground prepared by this polylingual, diplomatic Frenchman in the service of the Spanish government.

Also in East Texas appeared the notorious Philip Nolan, famed, with the usual literary license, for his role as the anti-hero in Edward Everett Hale's *A Man Without A Country.* Nolan's movements are almost as shadowy as those of his mentor, General James Wilkinson. Certainly from the time he was about nineteen years old, this Irish-born freebooter hung around Nacogdoches, ostensibly trading for horses with the Indians. Sometimes he seems to have been working for himself and sometimes for the French, who were back in control in Louisiana. Nolan made it over the trail as far as San Antonio, probably during 1795. By 1797 he was back again. Two years later, just before Christmas, he married a Natchez girl named Frances Lintot, only to leave her in less than a year to return to his first love, Texas. Meanwhile the Spanish, forever listening, heard of Nolan's repeated trips and wondered whether he might not be engaged on some sinister mission. Could he be inciting the Indians to join in an uprising to run the Spanish out of Texas?

As a result of this suspicion Governor Juan Bautista Elguezábal was receiving a flood of petitions of emigrants from Louisiana requesting to move to Texas. However, he felt that Texas was not ready to receive emigrants, but more than that, he feared what Nolan might be going to stir up anti-Spanish feelings. He therefore issued an order for Nolan's arrest should he reenter Texas. A defiant Nolan did that, just north of Nacogdoches, where he built a fort on Nolan Creek. He was killed, probably near Waco, on March 4, 1801, fighting the Spanish who had come to arrest him. He had been forced to live on the meat of his horses while he was on the run. When the Spanish caught him, they offered him a surrender, but he chose to fight to the finish. It was the end of the first Anglo-American to map Texas. Meanwhile back in Natchez, Frances Lintot Nolan, who probably could not have cared less for Texas, gave birth to a son six months after her husband had left on his latest expedition. She died convinced that Philip Nolan had abandoned her. The son himself died of tuberculosis when he was scarely 21 years old. The man without a country became a man without descendants.

And so time passed. At the Mexican end of the trail Saltillo underwent almost a dozen years of revolutionizing and counterrevolutionizing as Mexico sought her independence. On the other end, at Natchitoches, now Spanish, now French, now finally through Gallic perfidy incorporated into the land-devouring United States, General James Wilkinson plied his unclear plans for empire. The country between Natchitoches on the Louisiana side and Nacogdoches on the Texas side became virtually a no-man's land. Because the Spanish and Texas and their new neighbors, the United States and Louisiana, were unable to agree on a proper boundary, General Wilkinson and Lieutenant Colonel Simón de Herrera agreed on November 6, 1806, that the disputed area should be proclaimed a Neutral Ground. Although not even the extent of the Neutral Ground could be agreed on, it was wide enough to cause little difficulty. On the south the Gulf of Mexico formed a natural boundary as well as barrier, and the thirty-second parallel provided a tacit northern boundary

Settlers were not permitted within the Neutral Ground. Knowing both sides, one is not incredulous that both Spanish and Anglo-American settlers moved in. The Spanish and the *yanquis* cooperated to the extent of sending joint military expeditions in 1810 and again in 1812 to expel outlaws from the area. Finally in 1821 the United States received the strip as a result of the Adams-Oñis treaty. The treaty was almost an *ex post facto* agreement, for the Spanish were on their way out by then.

Before the Spanish left, however, a disappointed, broke plunger named Moses Austin had come down the *camino real* seeking a start. He had already dealt with the Spanish, having obtained a league of land back in Missouri. He gave his Missouri town a Spanish name, Potosi, which has come down to the present mispronounced, with emphasis on the second syllable. For awhile in Missouri it looked as if he had made good, but the panic of 1819 wiped him out.

So Moses Austin turned back to the Spanish, seeking again a new start from outside his own country. Knowing that the Spanish had offered grants of land previously to *empresarios* who would bring in colonists for Texas, Austin called on Governor Antonio María Martínez in San Antonio, was ordered away, and then chanced upon the Baron de Bastrop, whom he had known earlier in Louisiana. Bastrop persuaded the Governor to forward Austin's petition to the chief civil and military commandant of Texas at Monterrey. The result was that on January 17, 1821, Moses Austin received permission to settle 300 families within an area of 200,000 acres. Moses Austin believed he was back in business. But by June he was dead, leaving the details of the settlement to his 27-year-old son, Stephen F. Austin.

Young Austin was not elated at what his father had left him to oversee. A thoroughly responsible young man, much more stable than his promoter-father, he felt the need to carry on his father's enterprise. At Natchitoches when he received word of Moses' death, Stephen Austin went back to San Antonio to receive authorization in his own right. This time the plans were much more precise than they had been under his father's grant. Among other things, Governor Martínez told Austin that the Spanish could not extend administration over the colonists and that Austin must be the administrator.

By the time the first colonists began to arrive, however, the successful revolutionary Mexican government had displaced the Spanish, and typically refused to honor Spanish commitments. Back across Texas and on to Mexico City went Austin to receive authorization on January 3, 1823, to bring in families. The law was a general one which also provided means by which entrepreneurs other than Austin could introduce colonists, each receiving 67,000 acres of land for every 200 families that he introduced. In a sense the law established a speculator's windfall, but the upstart Mexicans had no other way to compensate.

Gradually Austin's colony built up and other colonies were founded. Most of the colonies were below the Old San Antonio Trail, or barely crossed it. But the activities accompanying the settlement of Texas by the Anglos affected all of the trail's route. A rivalry developed between Monclova and Saltillo to be the capital of the province of *Coahuila y Texas,* for instance. At the other end of the trail occurred the Fredonian Rebellion. In this latter incident Haden Edwards, of Kentucky, Louisiana, and lately of Mexico City, came into Saltillo to get a contract on April 15, 1825, to settle 800 families in East Texas. About 1,000 people lived in the area already, including many of Spanish origin. These people were to cause trouble, because in great part the Spanish had been haphazard in dealing property. Edwards in effect told these residents that they were on his land and to get out. He was tactless, to say the least. Immediately hard feelings broke out, as the Mexicans and the descendants of the early Anglo-Americans sent protesting resolutions to Saltillo. By mid-December 1826 the controversy had boiled to the point that Benjamin Edwards, acting for Haden, rode into Nacogdoches, carrying a flag inscribed "Independence, Liberty, and Justice," seized the fort, and proclaimed the Republic of Fredonia. Promptly the Fredonians divided Texas between the Fredonian Republic and the Indians, in return for Indian help in the rebellion.

But the Edwardses were premature. The people around Nacogdoches did not want to rise, they did not want the Indians as allies, and they would sooner leave than fight. The Indians themselves did not seem interested. So Edwards and the others petitioned the people of the United States to help, again without arousing any great concern, so that when the Mexican troops showed up, the Fredonian revolutionists had no choice but to flee for the sanctuary of Louisiana. It mattered little that Haden Edwards had made his move too soon, for the Mexicans felt that if Edwards would make such an outrageous attempt at revolution, then he must have Anglo-American support. The Mexicans won this time, but would the Anglos be coming back for another try another year? Was Anglo colonization getting out of hand?

The events in the mid-1820's through the spring of 1836 are too familiar to repeat in detail here. The Mexicans officially shut down Anglo-American colonization on April 6, 1830. They may have shut it down officially, but not actually, for people in the States continued to stream in. Those who came later proved to be less patient with Mexican inefficiency and with the strange ways of a foreign ruler. Mexico was caught in the frequent trap of a new country, with one side after another contending for power and the country "forever revolutionizing." It could not govern itself; consequently Mexico could not govern Texas. If you wanted complaints, you had plenty of opportunities to find them.

Finally the hotheads took over, helped along by Mexican excesses. Revolution broke out, San Antonio became a focal point, Santa Anna's army paralleled the *camino real,* and finally the seige of the Alamo resulted in the total defeat of Texans there within its walls on March 6, 1836. Santa Anna continued to the eastward, ran south of the Old Spanish Trail, and caught up with General Sam Houston, who promptly wiped out the Mexican army. Texas was now free to go her own way.

For ten years Texas struggled as an independent republic, a bit more orderly but almost as uncertain as the new Republic of Mexico. The subtleties of the diplomacy for getting Texas into the Union need not be looked at here. The inconvertible fact is that Texas was taken into the United States, that Mexico thoroughly resented it, and that once again the *camino real* was a highway of bloodshed all the way to Saltillo and the Battle of Buena Vista. Eventually Mexico, which had firmly expected to win the war, caved in. The American troops soon went home, Texas was in the Union to stay, and *el camino real* had lost its identity.

For several generations this situation endured. As new roads began to be built, the *camino real* often lay outside the more commercial routes. In the early twentieth century concerned people, particularly Mrs. Lipscomb Norvell of Beaumont, began a movement to chart and preserve the Old Spanish Trail. After four years of intelligent lobbying, Mrs. Norvell persuaded Senator Louis J. Wortham to sponsor a bill to survey the route and erect monuments along it all the way from the Rio Grande to the Sabine. The trail is now marked, the first state road built in the United States to commemorate a vanished historic trail. *El Camino Real* has probably seen the end of lively history, but it can look back on more than 300 years of events—sanguine, questing, speculative—along its international route. Better still, the modern traveler who does not feel the need to pursue the maximum number of miles he can punish his car and body during a long day can drive with history all the way from Natchitoches to Saltillo, knowing that his companions along the trail have been Spanish soldiers, Franciscan priests, outlaws of no particular nationality, Tennessee settlers, Indians both pacified and warring, revolutionists and patriots, and an undetermined legion of the sorts of people who make history. It is a road that looks back—a paved stretch of heritage that winds from then to now.

The Chisholm Trail
by **WAYNE GARD**

Illustrations by:
Melvin C. Warren

OF ALL the cattle trails that led out of Texas, the Chisholm was the most important. It carried by far the largest number of Longhorns and gave work to the most cowboys. It also was the most famed in song and story. No matter where he rode, the ranch hand was likely to sing:

I woke up one morning on the old Chisholm Trail,
Rope in my hand and a cow by the tail.

Feet in the stirrups and seat in the saddle,
I hung and rattled with them Longhorn cattle.

Like the other cow paths, the Chisholm Trail grew out of an economic need. In the era before railroads, it connected cheap Texas steers with Kansas markets where prices were much higher; and it helped to stock ranges to the north and northwest, freshly wrested from the buffalo herds. By bringing northern cash—much of it in gold—back to Texas, the trailing enabled the Lone Star State to recover from some of the financial wounds of the Civil War.

Of course, thousands of Texas cattle had been trailed out of Texas before the Chisholm route was opened. There had been drives to Louisiana even in the Spanish and Mexican eras, and in the 1850's there were long, hazardous drives to California to supply beef to the hungry gold miners. Also, beginning in the 1840's, there had been drives north to Midwest cities and railheads. In the Civil War, Texas herds had been walked to Mississippi to feed Confederate troops.

Although the drives began wherever there were surplus cattle and ended wherever there were markets, most of the early northward movement followed what came to be called the Shawnee Trail. This route had feeder branches coming in from the coastal plains, the Rio Grande, and the western ranges. It crossed the Colorado River at Austin and the Brazos at or above Waco. It led north through Dallas and entered the Indian Territory by crossing the Red River at Preston, a small town later inundated by Lake Texoma.

Leading north through the eastern edge of what was to become Oklahoma, the trail passed Fort Gibson and entered the southeastern corner of Kansas just south of Baxter Springs. From there some of the herds were taken to St. Louis and others to Chicago, Quincy, Sedalia, or points in eastern or central Kansas.

In 1854 the first Texas Longhorns to arrive in St. Louis were viewed critically. The *Intelligencer*, noting that they had been trailed about five hundred miles, subsisting entirely on grass, added: "They never ate an ear of corn in their lives. An attempt was made to feed them with corn and provender, but they ran away from it. Texas cattle are about the nearest to wild animals of any now driven to market. We have seen some buffaloes that were more civilized." Three years later a St. Louis stockyards man remarked that the Longhorns were "not fit for people to eat. They will do to bait traps to catch wolves."

In 1858 the New York *Times* observed that some cattle recently arrived from Texas "were barely able to cast a shadow. According to the opinion of the sellers, they would not weigh anything were it not for their horns, which were useful also in preventing them from crawling through fences."

Yet the Longhorn beef was improved by stays in feeding lots in Illinois and elsewhere, and drives over the Shawnee Trail increased during the 'fifties. In the Civil War trailing to the north virtually stopped, though some was done eastward to feed Confederate forces and a little to barter in Mexico or (secretly) to pocket federal gold in New Orleans.

At the close of the war, Texas was overflowing with cattle, many of them wild or half-wild. With farms and ranches neglected, most of the calves had been left unbranded and many had wandered off. The unbranded cattle, called mavericks, belonged to anyone who could capture them and stamp on them his mark of ownership. But often capturing them was a hazardous occupation, and the cattle were worth little in a day when many of them were slaughtered for their hides and tallow alone. Only trailing them to northern markets could make the tough Texas Longhorns profitable.

So, in the spring of 1866, Texas cowmen wanted to send up the Shawnee Trail as many Longhorns as they could. They urgently needed cash, since the Confederate paper money they had been paid as soldiers was worthless. They put on the trail that year an estimated 200,000 to 260,000 cattle. But when the herds reached Kansas or Missouri, many of them ran into trouble. Some were met by groups of farmers who had pitchforks or guns in their hands. The Kansans and Missourians ordered the Texans to take their herds back. Some of those who refused were beaten or whipped, and a few were killed. Many of the cattle were scattered.

The reason that the farmers in eastern Kansas and southwestern Missouri didn't want the Texas herds to go through their counties was that they were afraid of a cattle disease that they called Texas fever. The tough Texas Longhorns didn't have this disease, but many of them had ticks on their backs. The ticks carried the scourge and, after being dropped on bedding grounds, gave it to cattle in Kansas, Missouri, and Illinois. Some of the northern cattle died, and many others became so thin they were worthless.

With farmers blocking the old trail and with northern states passing laws to keep out Texas trail cattle, the cowmen in the Southwest didn't know what to do. At that time they hadn't learned that the fever was carried by ticks and that they could get rid of the ticks by dipping the cattle in an insecticide. So they looked for a new trail to the north, one that wouldn't get them into trouble.

While the Texas stockmen were wondering what to do, a young cattle dealer in Illinois came to their rescue. He was Joseph G. McCoy of Springfield. He and his brothers had been buying cattle and other livestock, including some of the cattle trailed from Texas, and shipping them by rail to Chicago and other markets. He had been hearing stories about the abundance of cattle in Texas.

Young Charles F. Gross, who had gone to school with Bob Lincoln and later had helped make a survey for an Army telegraph line across Texas, told McCoy that in Texas he had seen "buffaloes, cattle, and wild horses galore" and that cattle and horses were "running wild and waiting for someone to drive them to northern markets." W. W. Sugg, an Illinois stockman who had trailed Longhorns from Texas, also told McCoy of the abundance and cheapness of cattle in Texas, at the same time warning of the trouble over tick fever.

McCoy wanted to set up a new market to

which Texas cowmen could trail their herds without being molested or turned back. He thought of building a shipping yard near Fort Smith, Arkansas, from which cattle could be sent down the Arkansas River, but a shipping point in central Kansas, west of the farm settlements, seemed more practical. So in early June of 1867 he went to Kansas, where the Union Pacific Railroad, Eastern Division, was building westward. His first choice of a site for the new cattle market was Junction City, but the exorbitant price asked for land there led him farther west to the village of Abilene.

Abilene, where, much later, Dwight D. Eisenhower would spend most of his boyhood, was then a small cluster of a dozen log cabins with a log store and a hotel of six rooms. Most of the buildings had their roofs covered with mud. But McCoy chose Abilene as the site of a new market for Texas cattle. That summer he built stockyards to hold the cattle and loading pens from which they could be driven into the railroad cars. He also built an office, scales, and a hotel called the Drover's Cottage, where some of the Texans could stay.

McCoy sent handbills and other messages to Texas to tell cowmen of his new market. They could reach it by a new trail, considerably west of the old Shawnee Trail. As the new route would pass west of most of the farm country, the drovers should have little trouble. The Texans received this news too late for spring drives, but a few of them made fall drives over the trail to Abilene.

Most of the cattle taken to the new Abilene market in the fall of 1867 were herds that had been taken up the Shawnee Trail in 1866 or the spring of 1867 and had been cut off from the markets because of the trouble over Texas fever. They had been held and grazed in the northern part of the Indian Territory to await developments. Probably the first herd to be taken directly from Texas was that of O. W. Wheeler and two associates, who brought 2,400 head of Longhorns from San Antonio. The first shipment of Texas cattle from Abilene, twenty carloads, was started off to Chicago on September 5; and the event was celebrated in large tents with feasting, wine, speeches, and song.

The new trail, poorly marked at first, split off from the old Shawnee Trail above Waco and led through Fort Worth instead of Dallas. Soon Fort Worth became an important outfitting point for drovers, and its nickname was changed from Panther City to Cowtown. From there the new trail led north and northwest, along the line between Denton and Wise counties and across Montague County. It entered the Indian Territory at an abandoned Texas Ranger station called Red River Crossing. Through the Indian country it led past the future sites of Duncan, Chickasha, El Reno, and Enid, and on into Kansas just below the future Caldwell. Then it went past the village of Wichita on the Arkansas River and on to Abilene.

Perhaps the new trail should have been called the McCoy Trail, since McCoy started the market that led to its use. At first the drovers called it merely "the trail" or "the cow trail" or "the Kansas trail." But soon it came to be called the Chisholm Trail. That was because, in the northern part of the Indian Territory and in southern Kansas as far as the Arkansas River, it followed the wagon tracks of the old trader, Jesse Chisholm.

Chisholm, who was well known in the Indian country, had been born in Tennessee and had come west as a youth. His father was of Scotch ancestry, and his mother was a Cherokee. He had served the Republic of Texas as an interpreter in several treaty-making councils and had been a guide on various trips; but he had spent most of his time in trading with the Indian tribes. He had trading posts at several places, including one in southern Kansas, where the town of Wichita later was built. Chisholm died in the spring of 1868, without knowing that his name would be attached to the greatest of the cattle trails.

Texas drovers began pointing more herds up the Chisholm Trail as soon as spring rains freshened the grass in 1868. But not all of them used the new route. Some still followed the old Shawnee Trail as far north as Fort Gibson, then turned off to the northwest, up the West Shawnee Trail along the Arkansas River to the mouth of the Little Arkansas, where the village of Wichita was beginning to rise. The rest of the trip was made over the new Chisholm route to Abilene.

After rounding up their own cattle from the public ranges and, in many cases, capturing mavericks from the brush and branding them, the drovers marked the animals of each starting herd with a trail brand. Usually this was a slight slash or bar, most often on the left side behind the shoulder—in addition to the more complex brand of ownership. Sometimes several neighbors joined in making up a trail herd, each animal having the brand of its owner but all carrying the same trail brand.

Many drovers used one or two lead steers to help them manage the herd. Such steers were especially useful in starting a herd to swim across a river. They also might be handy in controlling a stampede, as in a case in Dallas, reported in that town's *Daily Herald* of September 12, 1873:

> The 1,200 head of cattle, except two, which passed through this city, taking the old Preston Road, stampeded near the residence of Mrs. Haynes. The two that did not take fright had led the drove from the time the owners started out with them and, during the alarm of the rest of the drove yesterday, stood motionless with the drivers, who had the satisfaction of seeing the frightened cattle eventually return and gather round the more composed leaders.

There were two types of herds—beeves or mature steers destined for the Kansas market and mixed cattle that might be used to stock ranges farther north or west. In charge of each herd was a trail boss, who might be the owner but more likely was a ranch foreman or a top cowboy. The duties of the trail boss were thus outlined by Bill Poage:

He must see that there are enough provisions, as short grub does more toward dissatisfying the cowboy than anything else. He must assign each man to his proper duty. He must be the first up in the morning to wake the men. He must ride ahead to see that there is water at the proper distance. He must know where to stop for noon. He must count the cattle at intervals to see that none have been lost. He must settle difficulties among his men.

The toughness of the Longhorns—descended mainly from hardy Spanish cattle, many of which had lived wild in the brush—made them well adapted to the long trails that often had wide gaps between watering places. But the men did not push the herd. They stretched out into a narrow string to avoid overheating; and they let the animals walk slowly, grazing a bit as they went along. They kept the herd headed in the desired direction but let the animals think that their movements were voluntary.

At the head, one on each side of the lead steer or steers, were two dependable cowboys on good horses. They were the pointers, and their job was to guide the herd in the direction chosen by the boss. At intervals farther back, in pairs, were the swing men and the flank riders, the number depending on the size of the herd. In the dusty rear were the trailers or drag men with buckskin poppers to use when necessary on weaklings or laggards.

In most outfits the men changed places day by day in a fixed rotation. The trail cook, who ranked next to the boss in authority, had charge of the chuck wagon, while the wrangler, often a young boy, kept watch over the spare horses and brought into camp those asked for by each cowboy. Each might have six or seven in the remuda, the spares to be sold at the end of the trail.

In the early years of the Chisholm Trail, as in the period of the Shawnee Trail, a herd might include only a few hundred or perhaps a thousand animals. Gradually the average size increased, some herds being made up of several thousand. But experience showed that a herd of more than three thousand was impractical, since a larger number complicated watering at the overnight stops.

Sundown did not end the work of the trail hand. After the herd had been bedded down for the night, the men, in pairs, were assigned duties as night guards. Usually the turn of each pair was two hours. The guards rode slowly around the herd, in opposite directions, crooning or humming hymns or frontier songs to keep themselves awake and to help keep the cattle asleep. "To ride around the big steers at night, all lying down full as a tick, chewing their cuds and blowing, with the moon shining on their horns," said James Benton, "was a sight to make a man's eyes pop."

The cook, often an old cowboy who had become too stove up for horseback work, might be viewed by the cowboys as cranky, but usually he did his best to keep them well fed. James H. Cook recalled that on the trail "a cook could do more toward making life pleasant for those about him than any other man in the outfit. A good-natured, hustling cook meant a lot to a trail boss. A cheery voice ringing out at daybreak, shouting, 'Roll out there, fellers, and hear the little birdies sing their praises to God!' or 'Arise and shine and give God the glory!' would make the most crusty waddy grin as he crawled out to partake of his morning meal—even when he was extremely short of sleep."

The cook's chuck wagon, which had replaced earlier pack mules and oxcarts used to carry food and equipment, had been well evolved to meet its needs. Gradually adapted from an ordinary farm or government wagon, it had axles of iron instead of wood, wide tires for better traction, and extra sideboards to hold the men's bedrolls. Its most distinctive feature was the chuck box at the back end. This closed cupboard, with spaces for food and utensils, had a sloping rear end that was opened out to form a kitchen table in front of the cabinet.

A water barrel usually stood in the front of the wagon. Underneath might be a rawhide hammock or 'possum belly for spare wood or buffalo chips for the cook's fire. At Matagorda a man who saw trail wagons being loaded in front of the grocery stores in 1874 wrote:

> The outfit of a Texas drover is a scientific fit. There seldom is a cover to the wagon—it's too much trouble. The whole is exposed to public gaze. There are kegs of molasses, jugs of vinegar, boxes of bacon, sugar, and a variety of other provisions. Some things are strapped to the side in a helter-skelter but perfectly secure manner. Sometimes bundles of kindling are tied to the hind axle.

The food was nourishing but without much variety. Eggs and fresh vegetables were rare, but always there was plenty of beef in the form of roasts, steaks, or son-of-a-gun stew. Occasionally there was bacon or salt pork. With every meal came sourdough biscuits and hot, strong Arbuckle's coffee, sometimes called six-shooter coffee by those who said it was so strong it would float a pistol. Often there would be dried fruit, canned tomatoes, or pickles. Pie and cobbler were rare. More often dessert would be molasses to be sopped up with biscuits.

The men ate while squatting or sitting on the grass around the campfire. As soon as the cook had washed the breakfast dishes, he packed his wagon, hitched the horses, and drove past the slowly moving herd to the spot the boss had chosen for a noon stop. The midday meal was light, with supper as the main one.

The trail usually was over open prairie, broken by strips of woods along the rivers and creeks. The drives had caused most wild animals to keep out of sight, though occasionally an outfit would encounter a buffalo herd and would have to watch carefully to avoid a stampede and to keep any of the cattle and horses from joining the wild herd. In places where the grass was badly worn from trampling or grazing, the cattle would be taken to one side or the other, thus broadening or varying the route.

Those drovers who came up from San Antonio or the coastal plains found the Colorado River easy to cross near Austin; while some used a ford just above the town, most chose a better one a little below, near Montopolis. The Montopolis crossing, between what later became Pleasant Valley Road and Canadian Street, was favored because it was free from dangerous holes and because there the water flowed evenly over a solid floor of rock.

Occasionally some unusual sight would vary the view on the trail. One such, in the southern part of the Indian country, was a high point called Monument Hill or Monument Rocks, which many of the cowboys climbed when time allowed. The mesa had a flat top strewn with slabs and boulders of reddish sandstone. To mark the trail better, early drovers stacked these slabs into two separate piles. Later visitors carved their initials or cattle brands on the rocks. From the trail a man could see the markers from ten to fifteen miles.

Although almost every Texas cowboy wanted the excitement of going up the Chisholm Trail at least once, the trip was arduous and full of hazards. No m atter how healthy and strong the trail hand might be, he could be struck by lightning or a deadly Indian arrow, suffer a broken neck when his horse stepped into a prairie-dog hole and threw him, or succumb to exposure in an icy storm. In the later years of the trail, unmarked graves along the route testified to the dangers of the long drive.

Aside from the peril to life and limb, there were many risks of losing cattle and thus robbing the drive of its profit. Sometimes, on either side of the Red River, white rustlers might drive off some of the Longhorns in spite of the Texas Rangers and local law officers. More common were the redskin raiders in the Indian country who tried to stampede the herds at night and escape with cattle and horses. As Army units brought the tribesmen under stronger control, outright attacks became fewer, but often Indian beggars and Indian taxes for grazing on tribal lands were expensive nuisances.

Often more costly than the Indian troubles were treacherous stream crossings, especially in times of flood. High water that sometimes delayed herds might also shift the porous sandbars that caught and sucked down cattle and horses. The crossings had to be made where there was solid footing on each side and at a time of day when a low sun would not throw glare into the eyes of cattle and horses. The trail hand used his most trusted mount in stream crossings and might call his best friend "a man to ride the river with."

In the river crossings, cowboys rode on each side of the cattle, trying to keep the herd in a compact and steadily moving mass. Only the heads of the cattle, with their flaring horns, were seen above the water. One trail man said they looked like "a thousand rocking chairs floating on the water."

The worst danger in stream crossings was that the cattle, while out in the middle, would become frightened by a floating tree or some unusual sound and would start milling in a circle. This churning, unless broken up quickly, would exhaust their strength and cause many to be swept downstream and drowned. Cowboys, at great danger to themselves, had to ride in and try to untangle the cattle and head them again toward the north bank. Bill Montgomery's outfit, in putting 4,500 Longhorns across the North Canadian in 1869, lost 116 cattle and three horses.

Quicksands were especially dangerous because they were deceptive. In a creek near the Canadian River, Mark A. Withers narrowly escaped drowning in six inches of water. "We turned the cattle loose there," he said, "and some would go up stream and some down stream. They wouldn't go right. I told a Negro to go across, but he said it was boggy. I rode in, and as soon as I got in the horse sank. Every time he'd lunge he'd go deeper. I got off and bogged down. The horse lunged himself out, but every time I stepped I'd go farther down. I called to the Negro. He threw me a rope, and I put it around my waist. I told him to pull me out. When he did, I left my spurs and boots down in that stream. I've never seen those spurs or boots since."

Once a few of the startled cattle began running, the whole herd would be up and off in an instant. Any wagon or tree in the way might be smashed to bits. Sometimes the cattle rushed off in a compact mass, but at other times they divided into bunches that headed in different directions. As a cowboy sang about it:

> Last night I was on guard, and the leader broke the ranks,
> I hit my horse down the shoulders, and I spurred him in the flanks.
>
> I popped my foot in the stirrups and gave a little yell;
> The tail cattle broke, and the leaders went to hell.

Those punchers not already on duty had to scramble on their horses and race after the crazed Longhorns. With the herd impossible to stop quickly, the men often tried to turn the cattle into a mill or circle to tire them and work off their fright. But the mill must not be allowed to become too solid lest the animals in the center be suffocated or trampled. "The steers could work off more pounds in a twenty-minute mill," said G. E. Lemmon, "than in a mile-and-a-half run."

It might take days to recover all the stampeded cattle, even when all of them could be found. Some might be driven off by Indians or mingled with other herds. In hilly country some might be found dead at the foot of a precipice. While riding after part of a stampeding herd on the Cimarron, Robert T. Hill and another trail hand had almost caught up with the bunch they were following when a nearby crash of lightning stunned them.

"My horse stopped dead in his tracks, almost throwing me over the saddle horn," Hill recalled. "The lightning showed that he was planted hardly a foot from the edge of steep chasm. A little off to one side, the horse of John Gifford, the other rider, was sinking to his knees, John himself slumping limp in his saddle. Just beyond him lay old Buck, the mighty lead steer, killed by the bolt of lightning that had knocked Gifford unconscious. The rest of our bunch of cattle were down under the cliff, some of them dead."

Although the stampeding cattle, if they could see it in time, usually would split and go around any firm object in their path, the danger of falling into the way of the crazed animals was something that every cowboy dreaded. Some had heard Mark Reeves tell what to do when unhorsed in front of a rushing herd. All the fallen puncher needed to do to split the herd, said Reeves, was to bend over, facing the oncoming cattle, hold his hat between his teeth, and shake his coat tails over his back. But there's no record of anyone trying that method.

From the start, the Chisholm Trail proved profitable with the Texas drovers. They took about 35,000 cattle to Abilene in 1867, and for the next four years the number virtually doubled each year. There were an estimated 75,000 in 1868, 150,000 in 1869, 300,00 in 1870, and 600,000 to 700,000 in the peak year of 1871. With the deluge of 1871 more than Abilene could handle, some herds were marketed at Newton, Ellsworth, and other Kansas towns.

Among the prominent Texas cowmen who took Longhorns up the Chisholm Trail in its early years were Mark A. Withers of Lockhart, a veteran of Louisiana and West Shawnee trails; Dudley H. Snyder of Round Rock, who had trailed earlier to Mississippi and New Mexico; Seth Mabry, who had taken cattle to New Orleans; Eugene B. Millett of Seguin, who had had trouble on the Shawnee Trail; and George W. Slaughter of Palo Pinto County, who combined cattle raising with preaching.

In August, 1868, when a new scare over Texas fever kept Midwestern feeders from the Abilene market, McCoy, with many steers at hand, devised two advertising schemes to revive his business. One was to take Illinois buyers on a buffalo hunt in September, on the plains to the west, followed by entertainment in Abilene. The other was to get up a Wild West show in which cowboys rode, roped, and threw wild steers and which displayed buffaloes, wild horses, and elk that his men had captured in August. The circus drew large crowds in St. Louis and Chicago in September and with the buffalo hunt, enabled McCoy to sell all his steers.

Fall cattle drives, although much smaller than the spring ones, were larger than usual in 1869. On one of those drives, George W.

Slaughter left his ranch near Palo Pinto on September 2 with about 2,250 Longhorns. More is known of this drive because one of the trail hands, Virginia-born J. H. Baker, who owned 480 of the cattle, kept a diary.

For the first few days the grass was good, but some rain was encountered. The cattle stampeded on the fourth day, but the men recovered all of them. After seventeen days they camped near Fort Arbuckle, on the Washita River, where they found good grass and water. On the evening of September 27, after turning off the trail for water, the men with the herd missed the wagons and had to camp for the night without them. But they found them the next morning, and on the evening of that day they crossed the Salt Fork of the Arkansas.

The outfit reached the Arkansas on October 1 and found the water low enough for fording without swimming. With the weather turning frosty, the herd traveled ten to twelve miles a day. On the 8th, Baker wrote in his diary:

A cold norther, with rain, blew up just before day. Continued to rain until 9 a.m. Norther blew all day. Some of the hands drove the cattle about four miles, while the boss, myself, and four of the hands spent the day hunting for a yoke of our oxen. Found them in another herd and got them back to our camp about sunset. Made camp on Rock Creek near the Kansas line. Twenty thousand head of cattle are being grazed in this vicinity, waiting for buyers.

On the 17th Parson Slaughter split the herd, planning to winter some of the cattle near the Little Arkansas. He sent Baker and five others on to Abilene with the remaining 350 head, where buyers took them on the 25th and shipped them the next day. On November 5, after swapping horses and buying a wagon, harness, and a supply of warm clothing, Baker started back to Texas.

Abilene visitors in 1870 included the celebrated showman, P. T. Barnum. He liked the town so well that he invested thirty thousand dollars in a cattle business there.

By 1871, when the Chisholm Trail was a beaten path and a bit safer, even some Texas women went up this cattle route with their husbands. Mrs. George F. Cluck of Williamson County, who took along three young children and was expecting another, rode in an old hack drawn by two ponies. Carrying a shotgun and a spy glass, she was ready to help defend the herd. In crossing streams, she rode behind her husband on a trusted horse.

Also accompanying her husband in the same season was Mrs. W. F. Burks of Nueces County, on the coastal plains to the south. She rode in a buggy pulled by two brown ponies and took along a Negro boy who did her cooking and put up her tent at overnight stops. She survived a hard hailstorm and a stampede; but she and her husband made the return trip by train to St. Louis and New

Orleans, thence by coastal steamer to Corpus Christi.

The influx of Texas cattle and their herdsmen quickly converted the village of Abilene into a boom town. Abilene had to provide not only food and lodging for the Texans but the entertainment they craved after a month or longer on the trail, almost bereft of social contacts beyond their own outfits. Although most of the trail hands were young, many in the early years of the trail were veterans of the Civil War. A correspondent of the New York *Tribune*, who was in Abilene in the fall of 1867, wrote of them:

> Here are the drovers, the identical chaps I first saw at Fair Oaks and last saw at Gettysburg. Every one of them unquestionably was in the Rebel army. Some of them have not yet worn out all of their distinctive gray clothing—keen-looking men, full of reserve force, shaggy with hair, undoubtedly terrible in a fight, yet peaceably great at cattle driving and not demonstrative in their style of wearing six-shooters.

After receiving his pay, the trail hand headed for a barber shop, a clothing store, and a place where he could take a bath. Then he was ready for the amusements the town had to offer. He tried the bars and the gambling rooms and looked over the sporting women, whom newspaper writers often called "soiled doves." In the fall of 1870 a reporter from Junction City wrote:

> Cut loose from all the refining influences and enjoyments of life, these herdsmen toil for tedious months behind their slow herds, seeing scarcely a house, garden, woman, or child for nearly one thousand miles; and, like a cargo of sea-worn sailors coming into port, they must have, when released, some kind of entertainment. In the absence of something better, they at once fall into liquor and gambling saloons at hand.

In addition to the bars in the hotels, Abilene had by the summer of 1870 at least seven saloons. The biggest and most popular was the Alamo, with a forty-foot front on Cedar Street. The three double-glass doors of its front entrance were always open. Its long bar had fixtures and rails of polished brass. Large mirrors on the wall back of the bar revealed the many bottles of "joy juice." Other walls were decorated with paintings of nudes in a florid style set by Renaissance masters. Although green gaming tables took most of the floor space, there was room for a small orchestra that played in the morning, afternoon, and night. Faro and monte were the most popular forms of gambling.

Of the dance halls, where a man had to buy drinks for his partner and himself after each dance, McCoy had a low opinion. Referring to their "wretched music," he added that "few more wild, reckless scenes of abandoned debauchery can be seen on the civilized earth than a dance hall in full blast in one of the frontier towns." But he added that the dancing delighted the lonesome cowboy.

Like the dance halls, the bawdy houses of Abilene's red-light district attracted many sirens from distant cities to relieve the cowmen of their dollars. Many wore fashionable clothes, and some had in their handbags a jeweled pistol or a dagger. Until the 1870 cattle season they lived in houses close to the center of town, but then local officials moved them to the bank of Mud Creek, at the northwest edge of town. Then in 1871 they were shunted to the southeast corner of town, where they put up shoddy houses on what came to be called the Devil's Half Acre.

John Wesley Hardin, the Texas desperado, was in Abilene in the summer of 1871. "I have seen many fast towns," he recalled, "but Abilene beats them all. The town was filled with sporting men and women, gamblers, cowboys, desperadoes, and the like. It was well supplied with barrooms, hotels, barber shops, and gambling houses; and everything was open." In the same year, Ben Thompson, a saloonkeeper and gambler from Texas, found Abilene full of footpads, pickpockets, crooked gamblers, and confidence men.

In an effort to bring order to tumultuous Abilene and to enforce the ordinance against carrying firearms, the town trustees hired in turn several marshals, none of whom could do the job. Finally, in May, 1870, they sent to Colorado for Tom Smith, a brawny Irishman who had grown up in New York and had been a policeman there. After coming west, Smith had worked at railroad building in Nebraska and had been a marshal in Wyoming.

Soon after Tom Smith pinned on his badge, people in Abilene began to notice a difference. When a cowboy rowdy known as Big Hank, who had a gun in his belt, began to taunt the new officer, Tom asked him for his pistol. After Big Hank refused and began swearing and boasting, the marshal felled him with a single blow on the jaw, took his six-shooter, and ordered him to leave Abilene at once and to stay away.

This action had a sobering effect on some, but in a cow camp on Chapman Creek it aroused a hefty desperado called Wyoming Frank. He began bragging of his prowess and bet that he could go into Abilene and keep his pistol in his belt. So the next morning Wyoming Frank went into town, and when he saw the marshal he bagan trying to pick a quarrel with him. When the outlaw refused a request for his gun and began insulting the officer, Smith backed him into a saloon, where, with two blows, he knocked Wyoming Frank to the floor and took his gun. "I give you five minutes to get out of this town," he ordered. "And don't you ever let me set eyes on you again."

When they saw what had happened, bystanders handed their pistols to the new marshal, who told them to leave them with the bartender until they returned to their camps. All through that busy summer, Smith, who neither drank nor gambled, kept order in Abilene, using his fists more often than his gun. But in the fall, while trying to help the sheriff arrest a murderer at a farm dugout northeast of town, he was killed by the wanted man and a neighbor.

For the next cattle season, Abilene had as marshal a less compentent but more colorful man, James B. (Wild Bill) Hickok, who had been born in Illinois in 1837. At 18 he had gone to Kansas, done farm work, joined the Free State Army, and in 1858 served as constable at Monticello. Later he had been a teamster in a freight caravan, a stagecoach driver, a Union scout and guerrilla fighter in the Civil War, and marshal of the Kansas frontier town of Hays.

Wild Bill, who had been written up in *Harper's Magazine*, was a handsome six-footer with a droopy mustache and long brown hair that reached his shoulders. He wore polished black boots and a hat with a wide brim. As a marksman he had a reputation that did not encourage lawbreakers to shoot it out with him.

Hickok, given more help than Smith had had, left most of the patrolling to his policemen while he made his headquarters at the Alamo Saloon, where, although he drank sparingly, he liked to gamble. In his home, where he took his guns to bed with him, he had several mistresses in turn; and in August he met Mrs. Agnes Thatcher Lake, who was in Abilene with her traveling circus. Mrs. Lake, eleven years older than Bill and widowed two years earlier, was an equestrienne, tightrope walker, and lion tamer. She was smitten by the marshal and wanted to marry him, but he put her off with excuses.

As a peace officer, Wild Bill did not have occasion to kill anyone until the close of the cattle-shipping season. On the evening of October 5, Phil Coe, a gambler, and other Texans were celebrating their impending departure down the trail. When they became rowdy, Hickok warned them to keep within bounds. Later, when they became a drunken mob and someone fired a pistol, Bill rushed out of the Alamo Saloon with a gun in each hand.

"Who fired that shot?" he called.

Coe, who had a six-shooter in his hand, said he had shot at a dog that attacked him. But Hickok saw no dog; and he and Coe, eight feet apart, began firing at each other. Coe shot a hole in the marshal's coat; but one of Hickok's bullets struck Coe in the abdomen, causing him to die three days later.

As the gambler fell, another man came rushing to the scene with a pistol in his hand. Wild Bill, mistaking him for another bellicose Texan, fired two bullets into his head, killing him instantly on the board sidewalk. Too late, the marshal discovered that his second victim was Mike Williams, a special policeman hired by the Novelty Theater. The crowd, sobered by the shootings, quickly obeyed Hickok's order to mount their horses and ride back to their camps.

For Abilene, that was the end of the business of shipping Texas cattle. Although Joe McCoy, by that time mayor, wanted to keep the trade, objections had been mounting on the part of both town people and surrounding farmers. The town families did not want to rear their children in an atmosphere of noisy saloons, gambling rooms, dance halls and brothels. The farmers, although some gained cash by selling provisions to the cowmen, were tired of having their crops trampled by Texas herds. So, early in February, 1872, a notice signed by local citizens and members of the Farmers' Protective Association was published and sent to Texas. It asked the Lone Star drovers to take their future herds to other shipping points.

One result was that Abilene subsided to a farm village, with many of its buildings empty and sunflowers growing in its streets. Another was that other Kansas towns began scrambling for the Texas cattle business that Abilene had spurned. The chief contenders, and those most successful in the next few years, were Ellsworth, about sixty miles to the west, and Wichita, which the trail herds had been going past about eighty-five miles to the south.

Ellsworth, first known as Smoky Hill Crossing, had grown from the crude blockhouse from which a small detachment of cavalry provided an escort for wagon trains and stagecoaches between that point and Fort Zarah. It had started as a farming community, become the county seat, and outfitted a few of the buffalo hunters. In 1870 it began trying to capture from Abilene some of the Texas cattle trade.

In 1872, Ellsworth, already a rip-roaring cow town with considerable shipping business, enlarged its stockyards, dismantled the three-story Drover's Cottage in Abilene and set it up in Ellsworth, and sent bids to the Texas drovers. Most of those heading for Ellsworth left the old Chisholm Trail at Pond Creek, in the northern part of the Indian Territory, and took a new short cut to Ellsworth, crossing the Arkansas River east of the dismantled Fort Zarah. Among those selling at Ellsworth that summer was the veteran Texas cowman, Dudley H. Snyder.

Wichita, so named because it had been the temporary site for a village of Wichita Indians, 1864-67, was at the mouth of the Little Arkansas River and at the edge of the free zone for trailing Texas cattle. The town became a trading point for the growing number of surrounding farmers, and its leaders began planning to capture some of the Longhorn trade they saw passing through to Abilene.

Wichita had a big advantage in being closer to Texas but had been unable to bid for the cattle trade earlier because it lacked a railroad. When a branch of the Atchison, Topeka and Santa Fe began service to and from Wichita in mid-May, 1872, Wichita leaders busied themselves immediately in building stockyards. They sent James Bryden, a Texas cowman, south to woo drovers and hired Joe McCoy from Abilene to go north and east to bring buyers to Wichita. In addition, they engaged a colorful Texas ranchman from the coastal plains, Abel H. (Shanghai) Pierce, to ride down the trail, with two assistants, to meet drovers and persuade them to market in Wichita instead of Ellsworth or elsewhere. The Texas business brought immediate prosperity to Wichita, which was building a new three-story hotel and which opened saloons and dance halls to entertain the Texans.

With more than 350,000 Texas cattle trailed north in 1872, Wichita outdid Ellsworth, shipping about 70,600 head, compared to Ellsworth's 40,161. Smaller numbers were shipped from other Kansas towns, while many herds were trailed farther on to stock new ranges. In that year Salina made its first shipment of meat in refrigerated cars. Another development noted by some was the upgrading of part of the Texas trail cattle, marked most noticeably by a shortening of the horns, as a result of the use of bulls of British breeds on the home ranges.

For the 1873 trail season, overland drives had a Texas railroad with which to compete. Dallas and Denison could ship by rail to St. Louis and other cities, and people in those growing towns had high hopes of a large cattle business. But the railroad had equipment for only a small fraction of the cattle, and its services left much to be desired. More important, its high rates led nearly all the drovers to prefer marketing on the hoof. Texans trailed an estimated 500,000 Longhorns to Kansas that year, compared with 350,000 for 1872. Most of the herds were of mixed cattle, with many of poor quality, as the stockmen wanted to unload while prices were high.

Although those drovers who sold during the summer received good prices, those who held until fall suffered from one of the nation's most severe financial crashes. The failure of the big New York banking and securities firm of Jay Cooke and Company on September 18 wrecked many businesses and banks and depressed commodity prices, including those of cattle. Drovers were left with herds for which there were no buyers; and again, as in an earlier period, many cattle were slaughtered for their hides and tallow.

One effect of this panic was to cut the 1874 trailing to about 175,000 head, or less than half that of the preceding year. But the quality of the cattle was improving as a result of better breeding. Many of the Texas cowmen were buying ranches instead of depending on the open range, and some were fencing their pastures. Denison built a meat-packing plant and hired Joseph G. McCoy to help boost its business.

In the 1875 trailing, which declined to about 151,000 head, the drovers began to feel the effects of the newfangled barbed wire that some farmers along the trail were stringing around their fields. But few viewed it as a serious impediment, and in Fort Worth rival agents of the Santa Fe and the Kansas Pacific (formerly the Union Pacific, Eastern Division) were busy persuading drovers to point their herds to their railroads. It still was much cheaper to trail cattle to Kansas than to ship them by rail from Texas.

Several developments marked 1876 as a year of change in Texas. Barbed wire was making inroads on the ranches and curtailing the open range. And the Chisholm Trail acquired a new rival to the west, replacing the earlier Shawnee Trail to the east, which had fallen into virtual disuse. At Belton some drovers left the well-tramped Chisholm Trail and pointed their herds to the northwest up the Leon River, then north past Fort Griffin, a frontier outpost that had become an outfitting point and hide market for buffalo hunters. Thence the new route, called the Western Trail or the Dodge Trail, led northwest to cross the Red River at a ford where Jonathan Doan had built a picket house with a roof of mud and grass and a buffalo hide flapping in the doorway. From there the herds were trailed north through the Indian Territory to Dodge City, Kansas, which the Santa Fe Railway had reached in September, 1872.

During the first two years after it became a railroad town, Dodge had been the chief outfitting center and hide market for Kansas buffalo hunters. In the first year of Dodge, 1872-73, one dealer, Robert M. Wright, had bought and shipped more than 200,000 buffalo hides.

Yet Fort Worth scarcely noticed the rivalry of the new trail, since the 1876 drive of an estimated 321,928 cattle was larger than that of the preceding year and the old trail handled nearly two thirds of them. Wichita had just lost out in the rivalry for the Texas cattle trade, since the Kansas Legislature had moved the quarantine line for Texas fever farther west, placing Wichita in the forbidden zone. As a result, many of the Texas herds, instead of being taken on to points on the Kansas Pacific, were marketed in Dodge City. To reach that town from the Chisholm Trail the drovers turned their herds to the northwest after they had crossed the Cimarron River and followed a new route to Dodge. In the 1876 season one of the largest cattle movements was one of 30,000 head, divided into twelve herds, which Richard King sent north from his vast spread near the southern tip of Texas.

By that time Fort Worth had become a roaring cow town, although herds no longer marched up Main Street, as in earlier years, raising clouds of dust, but were bedded west of town. For 1876 Fort Worth had as marshal tall T. I. Courtright, called Long Hair Jim, who carried two pistols in his belt. With help from several policemen, Jim helped to curb the ebullience of cowboys on Saturday night when some, after visiting the bars, were inclined to shoot out street lamps. Those miscreants caught were crowded into the two cells and dungeon of the log jail at Second and Commerce streets.

In the spring of 1877, as a Fort Worth slaughter house shipped its first carload of refrigerated beeves to St. Louis, Texas stockmen were recovering from winter blizzards, upgrading their cattle with blooded bulls, and fencing more of their pastures with barbed wire. More use of the new Chisholm

Trail cut off to Dodge City and the new Western Trail enabled that city to increase its dominance as a point for shipping cattle trailed from Texas and for forwarding other herds on the hoof to newly opened pastures to the north. However, the total drive of 201,159 head was only two thirds of that for the preceding year. Some of the herds had stopped in Fort Worth, which shipped 51,923 cattle by rail that year over the Texas and Pacific Railroad.

In Fort Worth, businessmen began in 1878 to take notice of the competition from Fort Griffin, on the Western Trail, in supplying northbound cattle outfits. For letting much of this business slip out of their hands, the editor of the *Fort Worth Democrat* berated the merchants of his city. "This drive is worth thousands of dollars to any city," he thundered. "That our merchants should have lost sight of the importance of having a representative to offset the influence of Fort Griffin's enterprise at Belton is singular indeed."

In 1878, in which the total year's drive from Texas rose to 265,649 head, the shipment of live cattle to Europe, which had begun earlier, continued strong, with cattle ships leaving from New York and Boston to supply overseas demands.

In 1879, heeding the advice of the *Democrat*, Fort Worth businessmen sent an agent, Dave Blair, down the trail to Belton to persuade drovers to stick to the Chisholm Trail instead of changing to the new one. The war was on. *The Fort Griffin Echo*, taunting Fort Worth, said one of that town's citizens, Frank E. Conrad, was ready to bet $500 to $1,000 that more cattle would be trailed by Fort Griffin than by Fort Worth that year. The *Fort Worth Democrat* replied that two Cowtown men would bet up to $2,500 that three fourths of the 1879 drive would use the old trail. Conrad sent a check for $500 to a Dallas bank but found no takers. Fort Worth would have lost the bet proposed by the *Democrat*, since, although it handled 135,847 of the 250,927 cattle trailed that year, to Fort Griffin's 101,010, its share fell short of the boasted three fourths.

The Chisholm Trail received a reviving infusion in June, 1880, when the town of Caldwell, astride the trail just inside the southern border of Kansas, obtained a railroad and, on the 16th of that month, made its first shipment of Texas cattle from stockyards still incomplete. Caldwell, so close to the border that it was not affected by the cattle embargo, was determined to outdo Dodge City. The latter, boasted the Caldwell *Post*, "had lost the cattle trade"

Caldwell, which had known the bellowing of passing Longhorns and the whoops of the cowboys since early 1871, was ready to give the trail hands the kind of entertainment they liked. It had several small hotels and livery stables and seven saloons, each with a gambling room. One saloon, the Red Light, also had a dance hall with an upstairs bordello that housed ten to twelve sporting girls, most of them brought from Wichita. Horse races were held outside the town every few days.

Soon lusty Caldwell had a place in the cowboy songs:

> We hit Caldwell, and we hit 'er on the fly;
> We bedded down the cattle on a hill close by.
>
> You strap on your chaps, your spurs, and your gun,
> For you're goin' to town to have a little fun.

Caldwell did ship more cattle than Dodge in 1880–25,531 to the latter's 17,957. Yet, of the 394,784 Texas cattle trailed out of the state that year, more than 62 per cent went up the Western Trail and some of those on the Chisholm Trail cut over to Dodge. The explanation is that most of the cattle taken to Dodge were trailed on north to Nebraska or beyond. The Chisholm Trail was beginning to feel the adverse effect of farmers' fences and, for many drovers, the slightly greater length of its route.

The 1881 drive, starting late after a severe winter, was smaller than that of the preceding year, totaling about 250,000. Both Caldwell and Dodge City shipped more cattle than in 1880–Caldwell's 31,644 failing to match Dodge's 33,564. From an 1882 drive of about the same size, Caldwell made its peak shipping of 64,000 head; but this was below Dodge's 69,271.

With Kansas quarantine laws becoming more restrictive and with barbed-wire fences narrowing the trails and threatening to cut them off, many Texas cowmen realized by the spring of 1884 that long-distance trailing was doomed. Yet about 300,000 Texas cattle went north on the hoof that year. Caldwell shipped 57,112 head and Dodge City 79,525. Caldwell, determined to match a popular bull fight held on July 4, held a rival fight at a Fall farm fair. But this was a flop, a reporter calling it "one of the tamest things of the season. The mad bulls that we heard so much about didn't have life enough to brush the flies off." The most exciting incident came when a bull tried to jump a fence, causing a mad scramble of spectators.

The 1884 season was virtually the last for the Chisholm Trail; and even Dodge, left with only one big trail, would have only one more prosperous year as a cow town. In 1885, cattle shipments from Caldwell were less than a third of those for 1884, and most of the stock shipped was from heldover, local, or Indian Territory herds. With barbed wire cutting off the old cow paths and with railroads reaching deeper into the Texas ranges, trailing, except on a local scale, was becoming obsolete. Off to the west of the farm settlements some herds still were trailed to Wyoming, but even that movement was diminishing.

In Texas many cowmen had foreseen this trend, and some had tried to find a way to keep one or more trails open. In 1883, 1884, and again in 1885, they petitioned Congress to open a national trail that would cross federal land and thus be free from farm fences. Opposition from Kansas grangers led the advocates of this plan to suggest that this trail be laid out along the eastern edge of Colorado. But Congress failed to act; and, although a fairly large number of cattle were taken up this unapproved route in 1886, the next year, with part of southeastern Colorado opened for settlement, brought an end to nearly all large-scale trailing over long distances.

By that time, barbed wire was blocking the old routes, rain and wind were erasing the hoof marks, and grass was creeping over the beaten paths. But the Chisholm Trail and rival routes had made a lasting imprint on the nation's economy. The trailing had satisfied a need for more beef and had enabled beef to supplant pork as the chief meat item on the American dinner table. It had provided beef for export to Europe, had spurred the rise of Chicago and Kansas City as packing centers, had hastened the building of railroads into the cattle country, and had given incentive to the development of refrigerator cars and meat canning.

Cattle trailed from Texas, along with horses and those cowboys who chose to stay, helped settle the northern ranges. The season of 1871, a Wyoming editor wrote, was "a memorable one in the stock business on the plains. Its success was doubted by many newcomers, but the year has closed with their unlimited confidence in the complete practicality and profits of stock growing and winter grazing. The number of cattle is double, if not four times larger than in 1869."

Having some of the trail hands stay on in Colorado, Wyoming, Montana, and the Dakotas, where their skills were in demand, helped to reduce the surplus in Texas. As trailing dwindled, the need for cowboys on the southern ranches was lessened by the building of fences, ponds, and windmills. Some of the cowboys started herds of their own, others took up farming, and a few turned to cattle rustling or other crimes. All would keep live memories of the long trail with its far horizons, winding rivers, thundering stampedes, and faithful mounts. The puncher might sing:

> With my knees in the saddle and my seat in the sky,
> I'll quit punchin' cattle in the sweet by and by.
>
> Fare you well, old trail boss, I wish you no harm,
> But I'm quittin' this business to go on the farm.

Yet he never would tire of telling about the Longhorn herds or the hilarious life he had found in the Kansas towns.

After it ceased to echo the bawling of cattle herds, the Chisholm Trail lived on in song and story and in an occasional motion picture. There were reminders in markers oet up in the three states, as at Wichita, where the trail crossed the Arkansas River, and Abilene, the first terminus of the drives. The largest monument was along a highway at the edge of Enid, Oklahoma.

Later a seven-foot granite marker was set up on the trail at Yukon, Oklahoma, and a large marker placed on the Oklahoma Turnpike. On January 7, 1967, a marker honoring Jesse Chisholm was dedicated at the Greater Southwest International Airport at Fort Worth. The unveiling was done by Miss Melinda Chisholm of Oklahoma City, a student at the University of Oklahoma and a great-great-great granddaughter of the man whose name was given to the trail.

Modern highways followed parts of the trail fairly closely, and through Oklahoma the cow path set the route of the Rock Island Railroad. As the 1967 centennial of the opening of the trail approached, the Governors of Texas, Oklahoma, and Kansas appointed centennial commissions to plan the celebration of this anniversary. Exhibits and celebrations were held in various places, many newspapers and magazines published articles on the trail, and a motor trek was made up the trail to Abilene, with Texas Longhorns carried in trucks.

The most ambitious part of the celebration, and the feature that reached the most people, was a special Chisholm Trail Museum set up in an otherwise empty passenger car of the Atchison, Topeka and Santa Fe Railway. This exhibit displayed cowboy regalia and guns, paintings of trail drives, varieties of barbed wire, and books on the trail. It was taken to many cities in the three states and was shown at the State Fair of Texas. Former President Eisenhower, who had grown up in Abilene, was among the thousands who visited this mobile museum. After the celebration ended, the Santa Fe exhibit was taken to Japan, where it evoked widespread interest. Thus, figuratively, the bawling of Longhorns strung out on the Chisholm Trail was heard across the sea.

The Santa Fe Trail
by **H. GORDON FROST**

Illustrations by:
Melvin C. Warren

THE CAPTAIN, seeing the wagon train was ready, gave the final march-command: "Fall in!" Slowly, the caravan began to move, one wagon following the wheelmarks of another until a thin, canvass-colored line stretched out for nearly a mile across the prairie, heading west to Santa Fe.

This 1831 wagon train was not the first—nor would it be the last—to make the journey from Independence, Missouri, to Santa Fe, New Mexico: a journey of joy and sadness; of hope and despair; of now-born life and occasionally agonizing death. Yet this much-used trail was to be known forever as one of America's greatest expansionist routes west, all falling into America's idea of "Manifest Destiny."

In essence, the Santa Fe Trail left Independence, Missouri, and travelled in a southwesterly direction across Kansas, the Panhandle of Oklahoma, and ended in Santa Fe, New Mexico. Where the trail crossed the prairies, it became a well-marked ribbon, sometimes a mile wide. At other places, especially through the Rocky Mountains, the trail narrowed to barely accommodate a single wagon.

There were four divisions of this historical road: from Independence to Council Grove, Council Grove to Cimarron, Cimarron to Rabbit Ear Mountain, and Rabbit Ear Mountain to Santa Fe.

The Independence-Council Grove division of the trail started in Independence, Missouri. Passing later-named villages and towns of Olathe, Baldwin, Burlingame, and finally ending in Council Grove, Kansas, this portion of the trail crossed well-watered prairies and was the safest part of the route. There were few Indians, and those encountered were of a friendly nature. These Indians, which belonged to the Kaw tribe, quickly became used to seeing white men, and looked forward to trading with them. The terrain was relatively smooth, being comprised of rolling plains, and when travellers crossed this area in the summer, they were greeted with fields of prairie flowers, onions, raspberries and gooseberries, which they often picked on their way towards Council Grove. About the only real inconvenience on this first part of the journey was great swarms of persistent mosquitoes. At night there was the constant hooting of owls and howling of wolves, but these were of no importance except to the untrained ear of the green-horn on the trail.

During the first leg of the journey, the animals were given an opportunity to work out their various aversions to pulling wagons and carriages. The unruly beasts attempted almost every ploy to escape their burdens. As Susan Shelby Magoffin wrote in her diary, *Down the Santa Fe Trail,* " . . . the mules I believe are worse, for they kick and run so much faster. It is a common circumstance for a mule (when first brought into service) while they are hitching him in, to break away with chains and harness all on, and run for half hour or more with two or three horsemen at his heels endeavoring to stop him. . . . One of the mules . . . scampered off. . . . After a fine race one of his pursuers succeeded in catching the bridle, when the stubborn animal refused to lead, and in defiance of all that man could do, he walked backwards all the way to camp leading his captor instead of being lead."

While not nearly as cantankerous as the mules, oxen contributed to the early troubles of the wagoners by straying off for water and grass at night time. They would often wander as far as the previous night's camping grounds, hindering forward movement as they had to be redriven across the prairie to the slowly moving train.

Making camp at such places as Round Grove, the Narrows, 110 Mile Creek, Ridge Creek and Big John's Springs, the wagon trains finally arrived at Council Grove, some one hundred and fifty miles west of Independence. Council Grove—so named because of a treaty enacted there in 1825 between U. S. agents and Osage Indians—was located where a thick group of oak, hickory, and walnut trees were clustered. The trains going though Council Grove would pause for a day or so to rest their animals, mold bullets, and cut replacement timbers for their wagons, which were slung beneath the beds. These timbers were to be used to repair broken wheels, struts, yokes, and wagon tongues. Since a small creek ran through the trees, clothes were washed and baths taken, as the pioneers realized that there would be scant opportunity for such things until they arrived in Santa Fe. Too, water casks were filled here, and the trunks and various other equippage which had shifted around in the wagon beds during the nine-day trip from Independence were rearranged with a more thorough knowledge as to the practical ways of packing for the arduous journey ahead. In addition, the members of the wagon made final plans for their defense, as the wagon master looked after security measures. When all was in readiness, the train left Council Grove for their next major stop, near Cimarron, Kansas, passing Larned and Dodge City on their way.

At Cimarron, the trail crossed the Arkansas River and proceeded in a southwesterly direction across the Oklahoma Panhandle, then followed the Cimarron River past Gary. Entering New Mexico in its northeastern corner, the trail passed by the well-named twin peaks of Rabbit Ear Mountain.

It was at this point that the travellers encountered a new type of terrain—the barren, rough, seemingly unfriendly eastern fringes of the Rocky Mountains. Here, progress of the caravans was markedly reduced, as the animals had to labor mightily in the rarified air to pull the wagons across the enormous hills and mountains. Although wagonmasters sent scouts far in advance of the caravans to find routes of easy access and traverse, the ground was still rough enough to impose extra burdens on the already weary travellers and their animals.

Leaving Rabbit Ear Mountain, the train slowly travelled to Mount Dora, across the upper Ute Creek, and the Canadian River. They rested at Wagon Mound, then went to the present town of Watrous, through Las Vegas, watered at Ojo de Bernal, passed through the small village of San Miguel, then continued through Pecos Village, up through Glorietta Pass, and entered the town of Santa Fe from a southeasterly direction.

Santa Fe was established in 1609 by Don Pedro de Peralta, first Spanish governor of New Mexico. A contract was made in 1595 between Don Juan de Oñate and Don Luis de Velasco, viceroy of Mexico, in which it was agreed that Oñate was to conquer New Mexico for Spain. Three years later, Oñate finally set out from Mexico City with an expedition of four hundred men, eighty-three wagons, and nearly seven thousand head of cattle. Entering the present-day boundaries of the United States at San Elizario, Texas, in the fall of that year, Oñate's expedition travelled up the Rio Grande and the Pecos Rivers, establishing a route which many conquistadores were later to follow. They were trying to find the fabled seven cities of Cibola, and the Gran Quivira, in which were supposedly encountered untold amounts of gold and precious stones. Oñate and other conquistadores never did find these legendary cities; but, based on reports of the vast, unsettled regions to the north, Mexico City sent out other expeditions of conquest. At one time, it was assumed that Oñate founded Santa Fe in 1605, but subsequent research has established the fact that Oñate's nearest settlement to Santa Fe was actually at the pueblo of San Juan de los Caballeros. Credit for founding Santa Fe is due to the efforts of Governor Peralta in 1609.

For many years, Santa Fe and Taos, a village to the north, slowly and quietly grew as the centers of Spanish expansion and commerce in New Mexico. In 1680 the Pueblo Indians, tiring of the tyrannical rule of their Spanish masters, revolted. Many conquistadores, their wives, children, and priests were killed in this revolt, with the survivors fleeing southward down the Rio Grande, where they established the villages of Ysleta and San Elizario, near present-day El Paso, Texas.

Recovering from their initial losses of the revolt, the Spaniards once more sent military forces into New Mexico and Santa Fe, and reoccupied the town; it remained in Christian hands from that point on. Trade was established between the Spaniards of New Mexico and French outposts in the Illinois country approximately ten years after the reoccupation of New Mexico, and both governments sent small caravans to trade with the Indians in that area, who were becoming more and more pacified. In 1694, three survivors—some called them deserters—of the La Salle expedition went to Santa Fe, settled there, and engaged in trading.

Commerce and life in Santa Fe maintained a mediocre pace until 1739, when the two Mallet brothers, leading a party of six from the Illinois country, entered Santa Fe and engaged in trading with the inhabitants for nearly nine months.

In 1740 various parties of French hunters and traders travelled to Santa Fe, among whom was a barber, Jean d'Alay, who, liking the enchantment of that village, married a woman from there and settled down to become a respectable citizen. Another member of this 1740 party, Louis Marie, gave the Santa Fe authorities nothing but trouble by thieving and acting in various ways contrary to the laws of the settlement. His career was ended by being sentenced to die in front of a firing squad in the middle of the Santa Fe Plaza.

Spanish authorities, alarmed at the increasing amount of muskets, gun powder, and other weapons which the French were trading to the Indians, began arresting many of the interlopers. Most of these Frenchmen were sent to jail in Sonora, Mexico, far to the south, where they would be held incommunicado for many years, and would not be able to lead French forces into the New Mexico country, as the Spaniards suspected.

The increasing amount of Spanish arrests in the New Mexico region little bothered the French, and they continued to journey to Santa Fe, some travelling to that area from New Orleans and other places farther north in the Louisiana territory. The route they followed crudely approximated the later established Santa Fe Trail. In 1750 Jean Chapuis travelled along with Luis Feuilli in an attempt to establish a route to Santa Fe and promote trade with the Spaniards there. Acting under the decree of the Viceroy from Mexico City that no more Frenchmen would be allowed to return to the French territories if they were caught in New Mexico, Governor Capuchin had the traders arrested, their goods seized, and ordered the articles to be sold to raise the money necessary to send the Frenchmen to prison in Mexico. The items were sold for 404 pesos, and the prisoners were sent south.

In 1763, the French-Indian war ended, and all French-American possessions fell to England save the western part of the Mississippi Valley, which was ceded to Spain. Some French traders and trappers continued to roam the Rocky Mountains, unaware that they no longer had protection from their mother country. In 1795, the governor of New Mexico, being apprised of the continued, but scattered, French trading activity, ordered that all of these traders be arrested and their goods confiscated and sold.

In 1804, Baptiste La Lande, a French Creole, was sent on a trading mission from Kaskaskia to Santa Fe by William Morrison, a merchant. Since American law was unenforcable west of the Mississippi River, La Lande is said to have kept Morrison's goods for his own uses as he sent neither money nor furs back to the Illinois merchant. Instead, La Lande informed the Spanish authorities of his presence in the New Mexico territory as soon as he crossed into the Spanish frontier, and this faithless emissary was escorted into Santa Fe by a troop of cavalry on orders of the Spanish governor. The deceitful Creole settled down in Santa Fe, married a Spanish woman there, raised a large family and then died without ever having repaid his employer.

Zebulon Montgomery Pike, American officer and explorer, was sent by the United States to the southwest in 1806 on a two-fold mission: to explore this area and to conduct a secret survey of Spanish settlements in northern New Mexico. After arriving at the site of Pueblo, Colorado, and discovering the peak which was later named for him, Pike sought the headwaters of the Red River. This fearless explorer crossed the Sangre de Cristo Mountain range of southern Colorado and entered northern New Mexico, where he and his men were met by a detachment of Spanish troops. The Spanish commander arrested the intruders, and escorted Pike and his party to Santa Fe, where the New Jersey-born explorer and his men were loosely imprisoned for several months. Pike and his small contingent were then sent to Chihuahua, Mexico, being graciously entertained in many of the small villages along the way. Pike was eventually released and returned to the United States, where he reported to his superiors about the natural and animal resources of New Mexico, along with special information concerning the military disposition of Spanish forces in that area. The young lieutenant published an account of his expedition, which almost immediately caused a great desire in many of those who read it to go to New Mexico for profit, adventure, and health. Pike's statistical descriptions of the land and its economy spurred the imagination of his readers, among which were many politicians and other influential Americans, who, believing in the "Manifest Destiny" principle of American expansion, began urging the government of the United States to negotiate for this vast area of land, whether by purchase, trade, or military action.

Although Pike's narrative was not published until 1810, three Missourians, Reuben Smith, James McLanahan, and James Patterson, guided by Emmanuel Blanco, left Louisiana on December 28, 1809, with trade goods for Santa Fe. The trio was arrested by a troop of Spanish cavalry under order of Governor Menrique when they arrived at the headwaters of the Red River. They were taken to Santa Fe and sent to Mexico, where they were imprisoned for two years. The prisoners were held incommunicado during this period, and friends and relatives of the men feared they had been caught and killed by the Spaniards. The editor of the Louisiana *Gazette* wrote in a March, 1811, edition of his paper that "three hundred men, well equipped . . . were expected to rendezvous at the Canadian fork of the Arkansas by the 25th of this month," for the purpose of effecting the release or retribution for the death of the three men, also "to bring off what gold they can conveniently seize." The expedition was never made, possibly due to the fact that the Spaniards had succeeded in aborting the 1810 revolution of Father Miguel Hidalgo to free Mexico from Spanish rule. The Smith-McLanahan-Patterson trio was released in 1812 and returned to the United States, where they made a full report to the governor of Louisiana about the cruel way in which they had been treated by the Spaniards. The report emphasized that the New Mexican peasants, in contrast to the Spanish officers, were friendly and sympathetic with the Americans and welcomed them wherever they went.

A trapping party, of which Ezekial Williams was a member, went to New Mexico in 1813. Williams became separated from his party on the Arkansas, and all of the others, according to Williams, were killed. The trapper cached the party's furs and returned to the United States, where he met Joseph Philibert, and the two men returned and dug up the furs. Philibert returned to St. Louis and told Jules de Mun and August Pierre Chouteau—the latter a scion of a great St. Louis fur trading family—of all that he encountered in the New Mexico territory, with particular attention being paid to the great amount of furs there. De Mun and Chouteau bought Philibert out and spent two years trapping on the Arkansas. De Mun received permission from the Spaniards to trap in this area, and then the Spaniards changed their minds. In May 1817, Chouteau and De Mun were captured and taken to Santa Fe, where the authorities confiscated their property and furs. The two young men were then imprisoned for 48 days. On release, they were given their horses and returned to St. Louis. The two trappers presented a claim against Spain for the loss of furs, their traps, and equipment, which was finally paid thirty years later by the Spanish government. The failures of Chouteau, De Mun and other Americans kept American trappers from working in New Mexico for some time afterwards.

In 1821, Mexico successfully revolted from Spain. For a short while, a very liberal Mexican policy existed in which trade and commerce with the United States and its citizens was greatly encouraged. Hugh Glenn and Jacob Fowler went to Santa Fe to get permission to trap in the Mexican territory, which they received, allowing them to trap on the headwaters of the Rio Grande.

Taos and Santa Fe became the base of trading operations in New Mexico. The Americans in Taos worked their way north to the Green River and the Utah territory, constantly seeking beaver and other pelts. Captain William Becknell left Arrow Rock, near Franklin, Missouri, in September 1821, with his party and an assortment of trade goods, which he intended to swap with the Indians for furs in the Rocky Mountains. Becknell's trail was one of the very first to approximate the later-established Santa Fe Trail, travelling west through Osage City to the Arkansas River. On the 21st of October the Becknell caravan left the Arkansas and travelled up what they described as the left fork of that river, when they made their intrusion into New Mexico through Raton Pass, and on towards Santa Fe. They were met by Mexican cavalry, which, instead of arresting them as the Spaniards had so many previous explorers, showed them the way to Santa Fe. Arriving in Santa Fe on November 16th, Becknell and his fellow traders were received with fine Mexican cordiality, the inhabitants treating them with every courtesy.

The traders' goods were soon exhausted, and in early December the five companions returned to Arrow Rock without incident, their pack horses heavily laden with Mexican silver dollars. News of their successful journey travelled far and wide, encouraging many Americans to enter the profitable trade with Santa Fe. Becknell's efforts won him the title, "Father of the Santa Fe Trail."

While Becknell's journey to Santa Fe was marked without adverse incident and financial success, others were not so fortunate. Thomas James and John McKnight organized a trading party, and left St. Louis on May 10, 1821, along with thirteen other men. McKnight went primarily to see if he could free his brother Robert, who had been imprisoned in Chihuahua, Mexico, in 1812. James had purchased $10,000 worth of flour, whiskey, gun powder and lead for trade purposes. The party set off for Santa Fe, going first by keel boat down the Mississippi, then up the Arkansas River to the mouth of the Cimarron, where they purchased horses from the Osage Indians, and set forth overland to Santa Fe. Proceeding up the Cimarron, then along the north fork of the Canadian River, the James party crossed part of the Texas Panhandle. There, the travellers were twice accosted by Comanche Indians—the second time by more than 2,000—who robbed them of a good amount of their trading goods. At one time, the travellers almost engaged in open combat with the Indians, but were saved at the last moment by six Spaniards riding through the Indians, who held them in high esteem. James and his men arrived in Santa Fe without further incident on December 1st, where they sold the remains of their once-large amount of trade goods for a total of $2,500.

Encouraged by Becknell's success, other parties journeyed to Santa Fe in the latter part of 1821, among which was that led by Colonel Hugh Glenn and Jacob Fowler. This group wintered in Taos, then dropped down to Santa Fe in the spring of 1822. Their trading mission was relatively successful, attributed by Thomas James to Glenn's converting to the Catholic religion for purpose of gaining favor with the Mexican government.

In 1822 it became generally known that there was little, if any, resistance by the Mexican authorities to trading missions entering New Mexico. Consequently, an increasingly greater number of trappers and traders ventured into this profitable area. William Becknell organized another trading party and returned to Santa Fe with wagon loads of trading goods—the first time such a vehicle was used on the trail. Carrying trade items such as cutlery, tools, notions and various textiles—especially calicos and velveteens—Becknell's wagons made the first legible signs of the trail that was soon to become so famous and important. This time, Becknell and his party were not so fortunate as they were on the journey of a year before. They encountered little difficulty between Arrow Rock and a point five miles west of Dodge City on the Arkansas. At this point, however, they decided to take a more direct route to Santa Fe, heading south across the sixty miles of barren country to the Cimarron. Ignoring the possibility that they might need more water than usual on this new route, the party carried water only in their canteens and relied on a pocket compass for navigation.

The caravan laboriously made its way for two days across the *Jornada* without extra water, suffering greatly in the intense early June heat, and encountering countless mirages of shimmering lakes and golden cities on their way. In desperation, they cut off the ears of their mules and killed their dogs, then drank the blood from these suffering animals, trying to quench their thirst. As Josiah Gregg wrote in his *Commerce of the Prairie*, "frantic with despair . . . they scattered in every direction in search of that element which they had left behind them in such abundance, but without success . . . but they . . . would undoubtedly have perished in those arid regions, had not a buffalo, fresh from the riverside, and with a stomach distended with water, been discovered by some of the party, just as the last rays of hope were receding from their vision. The hapless intruder was immediately dispatched, and an invigorating draught procured from its stomach. I have since heard one of the parties to that expedition declare that nothing ever passed his lips which gave him such exquisite delight as his first draught of that filthy beverage." Being refreshed both in body and spirit, some of the stronger of the party continued on to the Cimarron, filled their canteens, and returned to the wagons. The group journeyed on to Taos.

The Santa Fe Trail, like all other routes in the westward movement, had its places and moments of extreme discomfort and danger, especially in its earlier years. Since the pioneers of this trade route were not familiar with weather conditions the year around, several attempts were made to complete the journey in the fall and winter. One such was that which was made by Samuel Chambers and James Baird, who left St. Louis in the fall of 1822 along with a small party of men, all carrying trade goods. When they reached the Arkansas five miles west of present-day Dodge City, they encountered a heavy snowstorm and were forced to take shelter on a large island in the river. They had to stay on the island for three months, and most of their pack animals either died or wandered off. As a result, in the spring of 1823 the men found themselves unable to transport their goods to Santa Fe. Subsequently, they dug holes on the north bank of the river and *cached* their merchandise, then continued on to Taos where they purchased mules and returned to pick up their hidden goods. Accomplishing this, they rode back to Santa Fe, where they traded and sold the wares. The depressions in the ground which remained after the traders dug up their merchandise were visible for nearly twenty-five years afterwards, and passing wagoners named this place "The Caches."

The Santa Fe Trail was used but twice in 1823, and that was during the spring. A party consisting of thirty men led by Major Stephen Cooper travelled this route in that year, encountering many difficulties. Harassed by Indians—at one point Cooper's party lost all but six of his horses to the savages, and had to return to Missouri to buy more—and suffering severely from thirst, the group finally made their way to Santa Fe where they traded their goods for four hundred mules, then returned to Missouri to realize a substantial profit from this venture. "Their four-legged booty was apparently the beginning of the now world-renowned Missouri mule," R. L. Duffus maintains in his fine work, *The Santa Fe Trail*. "This notorious beast was a New Mexican product. He invaded Missouri from the west, filling a need which the rush of settlement into the river country was just beginning to create. From 1823 on he formed a conspicuous article of commerce."

Josiah Gregg recorded how important the mule was to the Santa Fe Trail: "This animal is in fact to the Mexican, what the camel has always been to the Arab—invaluable for the transportation of freight over sandy deserts and mountainous roads, where no other means of conveyance could be used to such advantage. These mules will travel for hundreds of miles with a load of the most bulky and unwieldy articles, weighing frequently three or four hundred pounds . . . . Freights are carried from point to point, and over the most rugged mountain passes at a much cheaper rate than foreigners can transport their merchandise in wagons, even through a level country."

William Becknell returned in 1824 with his largest amount of trading goods. This time, along with the usual cutlery, tools, plows, velveteen and calicos, Becknell brought other notions and textiles, especially large quantities of domestic ticking, grilling, and shirting.

Another group, comprised of eighty-one traders, twenty-five wagons, one hundred fifty-six horses, mules and other beasts of burden, left Vernon, Missouri, on May 16th. On this trip, the wagoners carried with them a small cannon to be used for frightening away Indians. The group suffered greatly from thirst on the *Jornada,* and some of the animals died. They arrived in Santa Fe on July 28th, where they traded off their $35,000 investment for $10,000 in furs and $180,000 in Mexican gold and silver pieces.

By the summer of 1824, national attention was focused on the Santa Fe Trail. Missouri Governor Alexander McNair petitioned Congress for legislation beneficial to the trail. Senator Thomas Hart Benton, favoring this legislation, joined an expedition to Santa Fe with the avowed purpose of personally obtaining information for the benefit of this bill. On returning to Washington from Santa Fe, Benton was even more enthusiastic about the trail, and quickly gathered support for his proposed legislation.

Congress approved Benton's bill, and two days before inauguration day, 1825, President James Monroe signed the bill which provided for $30,000 to be used in the trail's improvement. However, only $10,000 of this was set aside for the actual marking of the Santa Fe Trail, the rest being spent in purchasing rights-of-way from the Indians and other parties. On assuming office, President John Quincy Adams appointed a three-man commission to supervise the work. A surveying expedition left Franklin, Missouri, on July 4, 1825, and began plotting the official Santa Fe Trail.

Paralleling latter-day Kansas towns of Burdick, McPherson, and Lyons, the surveying party laid their official route in a due-westerly direction until they arrived at the great bend of the Arkansas River. There, they followed the northern bank of this great river in a southwesterly direction, passing Pawnee Rock upon which was inscribed names of the early pioneers to this area, then Larned, Kinsley and Dodge City. For a short distance they once again headed west to Cimarron. Here, the surveyors cut across the deceptive *Jornada,* intersecting the Cimarron River near present-day Kismet, Kansas. Following the Cimarron, the group proceeded in a southwesterly direction across the Oklahoma panhandle, passing Gary, Oklahoma, and entered New Mexico in its northeastern corner. Using the twin peaks of Rabbit Ear Mountain as a guide, the caravan continued on to Santa Fe.

Thus the trail was marked by government surveyors; rights-of-way were purchased from the Indians, and the Santa Fe Trail was officially accepted and so designated by the American Government. Almost immediately, greater emphasis was given to the importance of the trail, and an increasing number of Americans turned their eyes westward for profit, health, and adventure. In 1824, $35,000 worth of goods were freighted to Santa Fe. The following year, this amount was increased by $30,000 being accompanied by 130 traders and freighters. By 1828, $150,000 in merchandise was taken to Santa Fe in 100 wagons, accompanied by 200 men. With the exception of a few years, the trade continued to grow, as the returns on most investments to this lucrative area were great, with some investors realizing more than 600% profit.

As a result of increasingly greater numbers of traders and trappers using the newly-recognized trail, new settlements sprang up along the way. Franklin, Missouri, became the gathering point for those leaving for Santa Fe, but was replaced by Independence, Missouri, due to its more convenient location. Steamboats were able to ascend the Missouri River coming from the Mississippi and New Orleans, and were able to cut off days of unnecessary travel to the west. Mountain Men, Indian traders, and other emigrants made Independence their headquarters, obtained necessary provisions, and many engaged in their final "civilized" drunken brawls and orgies before heading west. Later, Independence was also to serve as the place of departure for those who were to travel over the Oregon Trail.

With the exception of three years—1829, 1838, and 1840—an ever-increasing amount of goods was freighted over the trail to Santa Fe, until in 1843, when $450,000 worth of merchandise was transported to the New Mexican settlement by 350 wagoners. The Mexican Government, taking note of this, began imposing higher and higher tariffs on the goods brought into Santa Fe. In 1839, for instance, Governor Armjio placed a $500 tax on each wagon. On learning this, American ingenuity made itself present, and the wagoners either had larger wagons built to accomodate more goods, or else, stopping on the outskirts of Santa Fe, the freighters piled normal-sized wagons high with goods from two or three other wagons, abandoned the empty ones and, overladen but triumphant, crept into Santa Fe past frustrated tax collectors. Soon seeing that their exhorbitant tax methods were of little avail, the Mexican officials greatly reduced the tariffs, and the situation was resolved. They reasoned that it was far better to collect a smaller amount of money for more wagons, than to receive a large amount for but a few.

During the time that the trail was becoming firmly established, an industry was initiated by the whim of fortune and fashion which was to play a major role in the development of the trail. Beau Brummel, English fashion plate and dandy, started a new clothing fad by wearing tall beaver hats in 1799. This new style was quickly accepted by men in Europe and the eastern part of the United States, and the beaver hat empire was created. Such men as Manuel Lisa and John Jacob Astor established powerful companies which employed many trappers and fur traders to get as many of the web-footed, industrious rodents as possible to supply the increasing demand. While the Hudson's Bay Company concentrated on obtaining beaver furs from Canada, Astor and his Astorians at first trapped around the Great Lakes region. Later, Astor and his men expanded their operations to the Pacific coast, opening up new and vast areas of the United States for further exploration and settlement.

While the Astor interests and explorations were concentrated in the north, a new breed of men was created in the American west, made up of independent trappers, traders and hunters, called "Mountain Men." Referred to by Frank Waters in his book, *The Colorado*, as "the proudest of all titles worn by Americans who lived their lives out beyond the settlements," the Mountain Men were of two types: individual trappers and engagées. The latter were outfitted by the fur company and received a percentage of the pelts they trapped. Such legendary Mountain Men as Jedediah Smith, Jim Bridger, Old Joe Walker and Kit Carson travelled throughout the Rocky Mountains searching for beaver. Many beavers were discovered in the Colorado basin, and trappers rushed in to get their share of the wealth. Since it took only 80 beaver skins or plews to make a pack weighing 100 pounds worth $500, the trappers at first did not have to work too hard to amass a small fortune in furs. Shortly after their discovery in the Rocky Mountains, these busy dam builders quickly disappeared from their easily accessible areas. Further explorations were necessary, and concentrations of them were encountered on the Gila river and in the headwaters of the Rio Grande, along with the streams around Santa Fe and Taos.

In the early years—from around 1810 to 1821—the trappers had to get permission from the Spanish governors of New Mexico to trap in that area. Depending on the mood of the authorities, these Mountain Men were either quite successful in their efforts or were arrested by the Spaniards, their furs confiscated, and imprisoned. Because of this capriciousness on the part of the Spaniards, all but a few of the American traders became discouraged from trapping in New Mexico.

In 1821 Mexico successfully revolted from Spain, and the new government encouraged trapping. Hugh Glenn and Jacob Fowler were among the very first to receive permission from the Mexican governor in Santa Fe to trap on the headwaters of the Rio Grande. Taos and Santa Fe became the bases of trading operations in New Mexico, and many trappers, falling under the spell of these settlements, married, had children, and became Mexican citizens.

As the beavers were decimated from around Santa Fe, the trappers worked their way northward to the Green River and the Utah territory. Since the trappers needed convenient, centralized places in which they could exchange their pelts for supplies or money, trading posts were established at various locations. In 1832, one of the most famous and influential trading posts in the Rocky Mountain area was established by Charles and William Bent, in partnership with Ceran St. Vrain in the vicinity of present-day La Junta, Colorado, on the north side of the Arkansas river. Called "Bent's Fort" by the trappers and traders, this trading post quickly became headquarters for mountain men in that area. Flying the only American flag west of the Missouri, this outpost was solidly built, having adobe walls four feet thick and fourteen feet high. The fort had turrets projecting from its diagonal corners and had loopholes provided in the upper portions of its thick wall, so that, in case of attack, the defenders might fire their rifles from relative safety. The fort had only one entrance, which was a square tunnel large enough to admit a covered wagon, and had heavy, sheet-iron clad plank doors at either end. To further compound security measures, trading windows were at either side of the entrance where goods could be exchanged with the Indians without their being admitted to the inside of the compound itself. The fort was always heavily manned, and was seldom occupied by less than a hundred competent riflemen.

The Bents dealt fairly with the Indians, and William helped matters greatly by marrying an Indian princess, thus assuring that the fort and its occupants would be free from Indian attack.

With the establishment of Bent's fort, an alternate route to Santa Fe was made possible. Many pioneer travellers left the regular Santa Fe Trail at the Cimarron crossing, and followed the Arkansas river all the way to Bent's Fort at La Junta, Colorado. There, the travellers would go in a southwesterly direction following Timpas Creek, dropping down through Raton Pass, then past the tiny New Mexico settlements of Ocate, Mora, and on into Santa Fe. Although this northern route was nearly one hundred miles longer, it was by far the safest. It provided the traveller with a constant, fresh source of water, and carried him out of the land of the Kiowa and Comanche Indians, who were almost always looking for small wagon trains from which to either steal, extract "gifts" for the right to travel over their land, or on occasions, to kill the unsuspecting traveller.

Considering the turbulent Indian country through which the main Santa Fe Trail passed, there were relatively few actual killings proved to have been committed by Indians at that time. Most authorities placed this number at eight men during the early history of the trail, although it is more than probable that some other killings were never noticed, or reported. Usually, Indians raided the trains to steal horses, cattle and other goods. In his *Santa Fe Trail*, Duffus states, "property losses, on the other hand, were often serious enough. In the year of 1828 they amounted to $40,000, or nearly one-fourth of the total amount of goods taken west from the Missouri river."

Josiah Gregg, chronicler of the Santa Fe Trail, recalled an actual Indian raid on the trail in 1840:

"Our camp was pitched in the neighborhood of a ravine in the prairie, and as the night was dark and dreary, the watch tried to comfort themselves by building a rousing fire, around which they presently drew, and commenced 'spinning long yarns' about Mexican fandangoes, and black-eyed damsels. All of a sudden the stillness of the night was interrupted by a loud report of fire-arms, and a shower of bullets came whizzing by the ears of the heedless sentinels. Fortunately, however, no one was injured; which must be looked upon as a very extraordinary circumstance, when we consider what a fair mark our men ... presented to the rifles of the Indians. The savage yells, which resounded from every part of the ravine, bore satisfactory testimony that this was no false alarm; and the 'Pawnee whistle' which was heard in every quarter, at once impressed us with the idea of its being a band of that famous prairie banditti.

Every man sprang from his pallet with rifle in hand. . . . Our Comanche seemed at first very much at a loss what to do. At last, thinking it might possibly be a band of his own nation he began a most boisterous harangue in his vernacular tongue, which he continued for several minutes . . . he suddenly ceased all expostulations, and blazed away with his rifle. . . .

Their yelling was almost continuous, breaking out every now and then in the most hideous screams and vociferous chattering, which were calculated to appall such timorous persons as we may have had in our caravan. All their screeching and whooping, however, had no effect—they could not make our animals break from the enclosure of the wagons . . . which was no doubt their principal object for attacking. . . .

The enemy continued the attack for nearly three hours, when they finally retired, so as to make good their retreat before daylight. . . . Their shot had riddled our wagons considerable: in one we counted not less than eight bullet-holes. We had the gratification to believe, however, that they did not get a single one of our animals. . . . "

Gregg made note that none of the defenders was killed and only two were wounded. The party did have "considerable damage in our stock of sheep, a number of them having been devoured by wolves. They had been scattered at the beginning of the attack; and, in their anxiety to fly from the scene of action, had jumped, as it were, into the very jaws of their ravenous enemies."

Kit Carson, famous scout, Mountain Man, trapper and hunter, along with his Carson Men, was involved in a fight with Comanches along the trail in 1838. Working on a contract to supply Bent's Fort with buffalo meat, Carson and five of his men were scouting for herds of buffalo in the southeastern corner of Colorado, one of the main hunting grounds of the fierce Comanche Indians. As the party was riding across a coverless section of this desolate area, a war party of two hundred warriors attacked. Calling to his men to kill their mules and use them for protection, Carson drew his mule to a sudden stop, jumped off, and slashed its throat, barely in time to escape the first fusillade of arrows. As the deadly missles thudded into the still-kicking carcasses of the mules, the Carson Men fired with deadly effect. Again and again the furious Comanches charged the besieged Mountain Men, but each time the Comanche horses smelled the fresh blood of the slain mules and panicked, swerving to either side of the small group, causing the Indian's aim to falter. Finally, seeing that more than twenty of their braves were killed by the deadly marksmanship of the buffalo hunters, the Comanches dismounted barely beyond rifle range, and began dancing in a death circle around the six white men.

One of Carson's men, captured and raised by the Comanches as a boy, cried out to the medicine man in his guttural tongue, shouting insults at the old Indian, implying that his medicine was worthless compared to Carson's. Carson nodded encouragement to his friend as the Mountain Man continued hurling his invectives at the Indian, shouting loud enough for all the warriors to hear of the *shaman's* impotent medicine.

Finally, the medicine man could stand the insults no longer. Leaping on his pony, he led the warriors toward the men patiently waiting behind their mule barricade. Carson aimed carefully at the onrushing medicine man and squeezed the trigger of his heavy caliber buffalo rifle at the moment the Indian ponies were able to once again smell the dead mules' blood. Seeing that his bullet had found its mark and knocked the Indian from his mount's back, Carson dropped to the ground with arrows whizzing harmlessly above. Leaping to his feet once more, Carson yelled his defiance at the surprised Comanches who had thought that their storm of arrows had passed through him unnoticed. Allowing their horses to rush unchecked around the brave hunters, the awed Comanches rushed past the Carson men into the desert, and they never again bothered the great scout or any wagon train guarded by his men from that bloody afternoon on.

With increasing Indian raids and hostilities, the wagon masters began changing their defensive tactics. Instead of stretching out in one long, continuous line along the trail, where space permitted it, the wagons—Conestogas, Rockaways, Dearborns and Jerseys—travelled across the prairies four abreast. At night, two defensive setups were utilized, depending on the experience of the wagonmaster: most often the wagons were drawn into a circle, but on occasions they were formed into a defensive square, and all animals were placed on the inside to keep them from straying or being stolen. With the exception of but a few reckless forays, the Indians left the travellers alone, since the warriors learned that such defensive measures were practically impregnable.

While the Indians failed to extract more than a handful of lives from the trail, death was an ever-present companion of the slow-moving wagon trains. Coming not on the feathered Comanche or Kiowa shafts, it often hit with sudden ferocity in the form of measles, diptheria, smallpox, dysentery, pneumonia and cholera. Calomel was the most often used medicine; many pioneers thought of it as being a panacea for all illnesses, and it was a common sight to see adults and youngsters, as one pioneer's journal described it: "... sittin' there as the wagons rolled on, looking out the rear all pale, drawn and calomel-ly."

Rattlesnakes, too, were a menace of the trail,

although their frequency has differing versions. They were "... proverbially abundant upon all these prairies," according to Gregg, "and as there is seldom to be found either stick or stone with which to kill them, one hears almost a constant popping of rifles or pistols among the vanguard, to clear the route of these disagreeable occupants, lest they should bite our animals."

While Gregg alluded to the numerous encounters with this deadly reptile, one of his early readers seemed thankfully disappointed when Susan Shelby Magoffin wrote in her diary: "And we also had a rattlesnake fracas. There were not *hundreds* tho', as Mr. Gregg had to do to keep his animals from suffering, but some *two* or *three* were killed in the road by our carriage driver, and these were quite enough to make me sick."

Perhaps the greatest menace to the travellers were the capricious whims of nature. As has been previously stated, the *Jornada*—that area between the Arkansas and Cimarron rivers—was noted for its extreme dryness. On occasion, however, sudden fierce cloudbursts would deluge this region, creating a quagmire. In 1834, the wagons which crossed this area left ruts which dried into rock-like hardness, and are still in existence. Occasional hail storms and "blue northers" assaulted the trains along the route, plunging temperatures while creating bone-aching misery, and all too often, pneumonia. In the drier stretches of the trail, the constant search for water not impregnated with alkali or cyanide was uppermost, adding anxiety to other miseries suffered by those on the route.

Indian raids, sickness, disease, rattlesnakes, and bad weather notwithstanding, the trail continued to flourish, with several variations of the route being made. One of these was the Fort Smith-Santa Fe Trail leading from Fort Smith, Arkansas, across Indian territory, the northern part of the Texas panhandle, and on into Santa Fe. But this variant, like the others, never attained the popularity of the regular Missouri-Arkansas river route.

In 1841, the President of the Republic of Texas, Mirabeau B. Lamar, in an effort to secure part of the trade being carried over the Santa Fe Trail for the nearly bankrupt Texas treasury, made an attempt to induce the New Mexicans to approve legislation to this effect. Lamar's plan did not meet with approval, so without Congressional sanction, he organized a military-commercial-political expedition in the last few months of his administration. Appointing Hugh McLeod as commander, Lamar issued a call for volunteers, and induced merchants to join, promising them transportation and protection for their goods to Santa Fe. One company of artillery and five of infantry were organized out of the military volunteers, and a total of twenty-one ox-drawn wagons were provided to transport supplies and merchandise valued at two hundred thousand dollars.

The expedition, bearing the official designation as the "Santa Fe Pioneers," left Kenney's Fort, some twenty miles north of Austin, on June 19, 1841. If for no other reason than various types of incompetence, the Texan–Santa Fe expedition was notable for failure. Encountering the Wichita River on August 5th, the Pioneers mistook it for the Red River, and followed the Wichita valley for twelve days when they were deserted by their Mexican guides. Hastily calling a conference, the leaders decided they were following the wrong water course, and dispatched a company of infantry northward to find the Red River. Finally, on August 20th, one of the company returned to show the rest of the Pioneers the way northwest to the Red River. Suffering both in morale and physically, because of lack of drinkable water, supplies, and harassment by Comanches, the ill-fated expedition continued in a northwestern direction towards Santa Fe.

Brigadier General McLeod and his scouts were unable to encounter an accessible wagon route through the Cap Rock area of the Texas panhandle. The Pioneers were divided, with some of the horsemen being sent to New Mexico for assistance from supposedly friendly natives of that area.

The band of horsemen encountered extreme difficulties on their mission, but finally met a small group of native traders on September 12th. While a guide was sent back to assist the remaining Pioneers into New Mexico, word was relayed to Governor Manuel Armijo about the expedition.

Near Tucumcari, the expedition was betrayed by one of its officers, Captain William G. Lewis. On October 5th, this turncoat persuaded his fellow pioneers to surrender their arms to the Mexican authorities without firing a shot. Although Lewis is given credit for this, the pioneers were most likely defeated by incompetent leadership and adverse plains conditions, which broke them down both spiritually and physically.

Undergoing many indignities, the members of the expedition were forced to march to Santa Fe. Their captors held them in that New Mexican village for a short while, then sent them Pioneers to Mexico City where they were imprisoned until April, 1842.

Returning from Mexico City, the newly-released Texans told concerned friends and relatives of the hardships suffered at the hands of their captors. Many Texans became incensed on hearing their account, and on January 28, 1843, Jacob Snively petitioned the Texas Congress for permission to organize and lead a retaliatory expedition against all Mexican traders on the Santa Fe Trail. Granting Snively's request, Congress turned the matter over to the War Department. A volunteer force was authorized, being limited to not more than three hundred men. In addition, there was a proviso that all spoils of war were to be divided on an equal share basis between the volunteers and the Republic of Texas.

A month later, one hundred and fifty men assembled near Coffee's Station on the Red River, elected Snively as their commander, and chose the "Battalion of Invincibles" as their unit's name. Snively divided the group

107

into three companies, adding a fourth as tardy volunteers joined the expedition enroute.

On May 27th, the expedition reached the Santa Fe Trail on the Arkansas River, near present Edwards County, Kansas. Eventually, they moved to the Cimarron branch of the trail, two miles west of the present town of Ingalls. Ranging back and forth in this area over a period of a month, the Invincibles finally encountered about 100 Mexican soldiers fifteen miles below the Cimarron crossing. A battle ensued, with the Texans emerging victorious, killing seventeen Mexican soldiers, taking eighty-two prisoners, while suffering no casualties themselves.

Friction developed between two factions in the expedition, and releasing their prisoners on June 28th, the Invincibles were disbanded, dividing into two groups: "The Home Boys" and "The Mountaineers." Immediately returning to the Arkansas, the Home Boys began operations in that area, but did not find any victims.

Snively, who had been elected to command the Mountaineers, led his men to another section of the Arkansas, where they encountered a troop of United States Dragoons on June 30th. Commanded by Captain Philip St. George Cooke, the Dragoons were escorting a Mexican caravan through United States territory. Claiming the Texans were in his country's territory, Captain Cooke told Snively that he and his men must surrender their weapons. Snively disagreed, claiming that this was Texas-owned property, and accused Cooke of being the intruder. Failing to amicably settle the argument, Cooke then had his forces cross the Arkansas, surround the Mountaineers, and forced them to surrender their weapons. The Dragoon commander then persuaded fifty Mountaineers to return with him to Independence, and Snively and his remaining one hundred and twenty men rejoined the Home Boys. Some of the Texans stayed on the trail for a fortnight, then joined the others in disbanding on August 6th.

Complaining that Captain Cooke and his Dragoons had violated Texas territory in crossing the Arkansas onto this portion of the Santa Fe Trail to arrest Snively's forces, the Republic of Texas filed a claim against the United States. Eventually the United States admitted Cooke's error and appropriated a small amount of money for the Batallion of Invincibles in the Snively expedition.

The day after the Battalion of Invincibles disbanded, Mexican dictator-president-general Antonio Lopez de Santa Anna, deciding that the *Norteamericanos* were creating too much violence in the area of Santa Fe issued an order closing off New Mexican ports to any and all commerce coming from the United States over the Santa Fe Trail. This order, while at first appearing to be a tragic death-blow to the trail, was remanded on March 31, 1844, and in the ensuing nine months, two hundred thousand dollars in goods were freighted across the trail to Santa Fe, being accompanied by some two hundred men.

The formal annexation of Texas to the United States occurred on December 29, 1845. President Santa Anna, still smarting from the

Republic of Texas' gaining its independence from him some nine years earlier, became thoroughly convinced that the United States next had plans of attacking, conquering, then including the Republic of Mexico in its possessions. Issuing orders to his generals, this despotic dictator declared war on the United States, and on May 12th the Mexican War officially began. While the great majority of fighting took place in Mexico under Generals Zachary Taylor and Winfield Scott, the Santa Fe Trail became deeply involved in movements of the Army of the West.

Being made up of practically all volunteers from Missouri, the Army of the West was commanded by Colonel Stephen Watts Kearny. Kearny was ordered by the War Department to recruit his army, take it over the Santa Fe Trail, overcome any Mexican opposition in New Mexico, then set up an American government there. Kearny had specific orders not to interfere with the annual spring caravan.

The wagon train which took the Santa Fe Trail in the latter part of May was to be not only one of the last civilian caravans for a while, but it was also among the largest, being made up of four hundred and fourteen wagons of various types, and nearly eight thousand draft animals, accompanied by five hundred and twelve men. As the train followed the now well-defined, hard-rutted part of the trail, Kearny started sending supply trains along this route to Bent's Fort. From twenty-five to thirty of these vehicles left Fort Leavenworth at intervals of three or four days, preceding similiarly spaced troop movements. Eventually, more than one thousand seven hundred mounted dragoons and an artillery battalion were on the march.

The troops were considered by many to be the rowdiest, most undisciplined soldiers in American uniform at that time. On several occasions, for instance, these dragoons slaughtered thousands of buffalo, contrary to the orders of their regular army officers.

The contingent eventually arrived at Bent's Fort in the latter part of July, and pitched camp near this important frontier post. Kearny was told by the Bents that they would meet with but little resistance by the New Mexicans, as they were considered to be friends of the United States. The Colonel doubted this intelligence, and remained at Bent's Fort, attempting to force his troops into a better resemblance of a true army.

On July 31st, James Wiley Magoffin, wealthy, affable Chihuahua and El Paso trader, arrived at the fort. Magoffin was a secret agent of the United States government, travelling on orders from President Polk to try to persuade the New Mexico forces to surrender peacefully. Magoffin asked Colonel Kearny for a small military escort, going under a flag of truce, to escort him to Santa Fe where he could confer with Governor Armijo.

Kearny delayed immediate action on the emissary's request, but on August 2nd, the Colonel assembled his entire Army of the West and proceeded to invade New Mexico, accompanied by Magoffin. Bugles sounded and drums rolled in a spirited martial air as the Army of the West left their encampment near Bent's Fort for the invasion of New Mexico, but unforseen difficulties were soon to be encountered which would make this one of the most miserable campaigns of the war.

A few miles south of Bent's Fort the expedition was first hit by one of the fierce sandstorms which frequented that area during the summer. The temperature continued to rise—one authority puts it to be 112 degrees—and they encountered fewer and fewer accumulations of water, along with little animal life. Three days later, the expedition reached the Purgatoire River and refreshed itself in the cold, rushing waters.

Resting only a short while, the Army took up its trek southward, pushing on across Raton Pass, while being forced to reduce rations to one-third of their normal daily allowance. "From that time, practically to the end of the campaign, the soldiers rarely had enough to eat," author R. L. Duffus states in *The Santa Fe Trail*. "And here and there men began to drop and die from heat, exhaustion, undernourishment, and camp diseases."

The Army of the West relentlessly continued its torturous way through the northern New Mexico mountains, and Magoffin, accompanied by Cooke, went ahead to meet with Governor Armijo. Along with these emissaries, Kearny sent a proclamation which he had been handing out at every opportunity to the New Mexicans encountered along the way. "The undersigned enters New Mexico with a large military force, for the purpose of seeking union with and ameliorating the condition of its inhabitants," the message read. "This he does under instructions from his Government, and with assurance that he will be amply sustained in the accomplishment of this object. It is enjoined on the citizens of New Mexico to remain quietly at their homes and pursue their peaceful avocations. So long as they continue in such pursuits they will not be interfered with by the American army, but will be respected and protected in their rights, both civil and religious. All who take up arms against the Government of the United States will be regarded as enemies and treated accordingly."

On August 12th, Magoffin and Cooke arrived in Santa Fe carrying a flag of truce. Cooke went to the Governor's Palace where he delivered Kearny's ultimatum and waited for a reply, while Magoffin visited Colonel Diego Archuleta second in command to Armijo. It is assumed that Magoffin persuaded Archuleta to lead a revolt against Armijo, telling him that if he did so he could establish himself as Governor of New Mexico, as the United States desired only to annex that territory from the Rio Grande eastward to the Missouri border. Archuleta accepted Magoffin's proposal, and persuaded all but a handful of the Governor's troops to disaffect. Realizing that it would be senseless to remain, Armijo hastily fled south to Chihuahua, after sending an ambiguous challenge to the invading American general. "You have notified me that you intend to take possession of the country I govern," the message read. "The people of the country have risen en masse in my defense. If you take the country, it will be because you prove the strongest in battle. I suggest to you that you stop at the Sapello and I will march to the Vegas. We will meet and negotiate on the plains between them."

In the meantime, Colonel Kearny had received no word from either Cooke or Magoffin, so he led his ragged army south from Raton Pass to the Canadian River, taking some twelve days. There, he learned of his promotion to Lieutenant General, while receiving Armijo's message.

Preparing his troops for battle, Kearny then marched south to Las Vegas, encountered no opposition there, and on the 18th of August triumphantly entered Santa Fe. He was met by Magoffin and Cooke, who told him of the capitulation, and that evening the new lieutenant general and his officers were grandly entertained by Lieutenant-Governor Vigil. The American flag was raised for the first time in New Mexico territory.

At first, all the citizens of Santa Fe received the triumphant Army of the West with the cordiality for which that town is noted. *Bailes* were held for the enlisted men, and their officers were entertained in private homes. After spending a month in Santa Fe, General Kearny decided the time had come to appoint a civil government, then carry his campaign to California. On September 22nd, Charles Bent was appointed governor and Vigil was allowed to remain as his lieutenant. Being satisfied with his appointments, Kearny left Santa Fe on September 25th with 300 of his dragoons for California, where he was to achieve fame in his campaigns there.

While Kearny was satisfied, others in Santa Fe were not, especially Diego Archuleta. This quick-tempered New Mexican felt he had been betrayed by the Yankees, as Magoffin had promised him at least the lieutenant-governorship for leading the successful revolt against Armijo. In addition, the rowdy Missourians had been taking extreme liberties with the Santa Fe women—married and otherwise—which caused the men of that town to build up an undying hatred for the *gringos.*

After Kearny's departure, conditions in and around Santa Fe continued to worsen. The remainder of the bawdy Missourians continued their seductions of the Mexican women, and began forcing their attentions on the Pueblo squaws, causing hostility with the braves. Englishman George Frederick Augustus Ruxton, author of *In the Old West,* gives us a contemporary view of conditions in Santa Fe at that time when he stated: "Crowds of [Missouri] volunteers filled the streets, brawling and boasting, but never fighting. Mexicans, wrapped in *zarapes,* scowled upon them as they passed. . . . Under the *portales* were numerous monte tables, surrounded by Mexicans and Americans. Every other house was a grocery, as they called a gin or whiskey shop, continuously disgorging reeling, drunken men, and everywhere filth

111

and dirt reigned triumphant."

Diego Archuleta, still bitterly unforgiving of the *gringos* for their failure to name him as Lieutenant-Governor, gathered some friends and went to Taos, where, assisted with liberal amounts of whiskey, they made plans with the Pueblo braves to revolt against the Americans on Christmas Eve. The Americans discovered the plot in time to stop it, but were unsuccessful in their attempt to capture Archuleta, who fled to Chihuahua. Although the revolt failed, hostility among the Indians for the whites prevailed and intensified as the Missourians continued their carousing.

Although the Governor's Palace was in Santa Fe, Charles Bent preferred to remain at his home in Taos, and when rumors were brought to him of an impending Indian revolt, he dismissed them as being false. The rumors continued to grow, and on the 18th of January, 1847, Bent received warnings from his New Mexican friends that bloodshed was imminent. Adamantly refusing to take their advice and escape with his family, the Governor informed his friends that their fears were groundless, and that he would stay home while they got out of the area. This was to be a fatal mistake on the Governor's part.

Pueblo braves crowded into Taos all day on the 18th to drink the free whiskey and listen to speeches being made against the *gringos*. As the day wore on, consumption of the whiskey and the Indians' hatred increased. That night, large bonfires were built to ward off the cold, and ancient chants and warwhoops resounded from building to building, and street to street, with an ever-increasing frequency and hostility in tone. The drinking, dancing, orating, and defiant yelling lasted until well into the morning of the next day.

Governor Charles Bent was awakened early on the cold morning of January 19th by a loyal servant, who told him of a large crowd of drunken, noisy Indians gathered in front of his house. Bent hurriedly dressed, then went through the front door to the veranda, where he faced the unruly mob. At first, there was silence, then one Indian began to shout at the *gringo* governor, and another, then another until the entire mob was shrieking their complaints and insults. Bravely, Bent tried to reason with the drunken braves, but saw that his pleadings and arguments were of no avail. The governor turned and tried to flee to the safety of his well-built home, but it was too late, as a shot from the crowd knocked him to his knees. While Bent's wife and children looked on in horror, other Indians leapt upon the governor, repeatedly stabbing him. One of the braves took hold of his hair in one hand and brutally scalped the still-living peacemaker with the other. While the Indians were occupied in mutilating Governor Bent's body, a brave Mexican lady helped his family and two other women, including Kit Carson's wife, to escape.

The violent revolt continued for five more days, during which twelve other persons were killed in the area around Taos. In Mora, the small, thriving village to the north of Taos, nine traders were killed, and for a while it looked as if the citizens of Santa Fe were going to suffer the same fate.

The insurgents began suffering merciless defeats on January 24th, when a group of three hundred fifty-three Missouri volunteer troops, commanded by a Colonel Price, defeated them at nearby La Cañada de Santa Cruz. The Indians retreated to Embudo, where Price and his men once again defeated them. The insurgents then fled back to Taos, and barricaded themselves in an old adobe church, where the Americans vented their fury on February 4th, killing one hundred fifty Pueblo braves, along with a few disgruntled New Mexicans, at a loss of seven Americans. Leaving the ruins of the church as a reminder to any others who might have rebellious ideas, Colonel Price successfully ended resistance in that area.

Although the fighting around Taos and Santa Fe was over, many clashes occurred along the Santa Fe Trail between travellers and the plains Indians for the next three months. It is well-substantiated that the Indians were often led in their raids by Manuel Cortez, a former Mora resident. Virtually every wagon train passing over the Santa Fe Trail was attacked, resulting in the loss of forty-seven American lives, three hundred and thirty wagons, and some sixty-five hundred head of stock. Bent's Fort was attacked for the first time, as were various military units on the trail, Apache, Pawnee, Cheyenne and Navajoes began vicious attacks on wagon trains and settlements along the trail, successfully cutting off practically all commerce to Santa Fe.

When gold was discovered in California, there was a great temptation to use the Santa Fe Trail as one of the main routes to that area, but due to the Indian trouble, all but a few of the bravest forty-niners stayed away, taking a safer route west, such as the lower land route through El Paso and Tucson, or going by water around the tip of South America. Also, because of the Indian uprising, one of the trail's landmarks was removed in August, 1849, when William Bent blew up the fort which he and his slain brother Charles had established some fifteen years previously.

Since government forces were in active operation against the Indians, they had to be kept well-supplied with ammunition, food and other provisions, so the government continued sending heavily guarded caravans across the trail to newly constructed forts along the route. A few merchant's caravans accompanied the government supply trains, but travel along the trail was markedly reduced from that of previous years.

The idea of civilians travelling along the trail, however, was not completely abandoned during the Indian troubles. In 1849 a monthly stage left Independence for Santa Fe, being advertised as carrying eight passengers and mail, and guarded by eight heavily armed employees of the stage, "ready, in case of attack to discharge 136 shots without having to reload." Although the stage proprietors assured prospective passengers as to the absolute safety of travelling in their vehicles across the trail to Santa Fe, there were but few passengers until three years later, when the Indian troubles had considerably subsided.

In 1850 one tragedy occurred which, doubtlessly, severely affected the stagecoach enterprise. A wagon train, led by Alexander Majors, was slowly making its way westward over the trail to Santa Fe when Indians attacked them at 110 Mile Creek, running off all their oxen. Although there had been serious trouble with the Indians west of this area, this was the first unpleasant confrontation with the red-skinned braves on the eastern side of Council Grove. After seeing to the safety of all members of his wagon train, Alexander Majors rode off alone and unarmed after the war party, catching up with them in several hours. The Indians were surprised and awed by this young wagonmaster's actions, and allowed him to return to the train with all but one of the stolen oxen. Starting once again for Santa Fe, the wagon train continued along the trail, and several days further on were passed by a stagecoach on it's way to Santa Fe from Fort Leavenworth carrying ten men. The wagoners in Major's caravan shouted greetings and waved at the swiftly moving stagecoach passengers, and watched them disappear to the west, a small cloud of dust marking their route. Little did they realize it, but the wagoners were once again to see this stagecoach and it's occupants, but in a far more grisly setting.

Major's wagoners continued their slow plodding along the trail for many more days, until, near Wagon Mound, New Mexico, they discovered skeletons of the ten men, their once swift-moving horses, and charred remains of the stagecoach which had been carrying them to Santa Fe. The wagoners buried the men's skeletons and continued on into Santa Fe without incident, where they told their sad news. Many years later, the tale of the fight at Wagon Mound was related by Indians who had participated in the affair: an Apache war party attacked the stagecoach at Wagon Mound, and at first the heavily armed whites were able to successfully resist them for an entire day. Two of the defenders were wounded and placed inside the stagecoach, and the rest, using the bodies of their dead horses as protection, continued the fight. Using every tactic at their command, the Apaches were unsuccessful in inflicting further casualties. That evening, a band of Ute braves rode up, and together the two Indian war parties were successful in massacring the greatly outnumbered whites on the morning of the next day. There were other attacks on stagecoaches and wagon trains, but none were as successfully brutal as this—the Wagon Mound Massacre.

With the decline of Indian troubles—for a brief period, at least—commerce on the trail began to increase once more. In 1855, more than five million dollars worth of goods were taken along the Trail to Santa Fe. Five years later, 9,084 men were employed to freight over sixteen million pounds of merchandise over the trail using 27,920 oxen, along with 6,147 mules, to do the job. This continued until the outbreak of the Civil War.

Originating in a slave state, the Santa Fe Trail crossed, for the most part, free states. Sympathies of the travellers were quite divided concerning the question of secession, but the New Mexicans were mostly in sympathy with the Confederate cause. Memories of the ill treatment by American soldiers which led to the rebellion of 1847 were still rife, and there was also the possibility that if the South were successful in their secessionist movement, New Mexico might become an independent country. While this was an advantage to the Confederacy, the fact that Union outposts in New Mexico were being invaded by an army of Confederate Texans was a definite disadvantage. The New Mexicans had mistrusted almost all Texans ever since the Texas-Santa Fe Expedition in 1841; too, the rowdy barroom behaviour of many Texas cowboys who chanced to visit Santa Fe, Taos or other New Mexican towns on occasion had not improved the situation either. Notwithstanding the Confederate sympathies, the anti-Texas sentiment helped to neutralize most active New Mexican aid, and possibly contributed to the eventual defeat of all Confederate forces in New Mexico.

The Confederate stay in New Mexico was of relatively short duration, although by February, 1862, almost one half of the twelve hundred loyal Union soldiers in New Mexico had been captured by Southern forces under Brigadier General H. H. Sibley. The rebels continued their victorious advance up the Rio Grande, capturing Santa Fe and Albuquerque, until Fort Union was the only remaining Union outpost. On March 11th, a small force of volunteers from Denver reached Fort Union, and this enlarged Yankee garrison succeeded in defeating Confederate troops in several engagements. The Confederates at first retired to Santa Fe, then, travelling down the Rio Grande Valley, forever withdrew from New Mexico.

Throughout the Civil War, the Santa Fe Trail continued to grow in importance as a major military route to the west. New forts were constructed along the way, and each day saw an increasing amount of Union soldiers on the move, going from Missouri to Santa Fe, or vice versa, as war situations dictated. Since the United States' attention was focused on the conflict elsewhere, there were several instances of wagon trains being viciously attacked during the years of the Civil war, and on one occasion all but one member of a caravan was killed.

In addition, guerillas, described by Duffus as that "riff-raff of the border—insanely cruel—representing no honest cause," attacked many settlements along the Santa Fe Trail, mercilessly killing, pillaging and burning houses of the defenseless civilians. As a result of Indian raids and guerilla activities, more and more Union troops were sent to patrol the trail, and by the end of the Civil War, the sight of blue-clad soldiers along the trail was a common occurrence.

Immediately after the end of the Civil War, the trail was deluged with travellers—mostly ex-army men and their families heading west to take advantage of new opportunities offered them in lands untouched by the horrors of the War. In addition, more and more soldiers were being sent to the west to fight the unruly Indians, and in 1865 three thousand wagons loaded with merchandise for Santa Fe went over the trail. Increasing numbers of towns were constructed along the route, and many stagecoaches were daily passing the still slow-moving wagon trains bound for Santa Fe. In 1866, some five thousand merchandise-loaded wagons made the trek, as did thousands of passengers being carried by the various stage lines.

Although 1866 was the Santa Fe Trail's best year, it also marked the beginning of the end for this great western thoroughfare. In 1863, the Kansas-Pacific Railway system began at a point near Kansas City. Successfully resisting multiple Indian attacks, adverse weather conditions, train wrecks, and the Civil War, this line had reached the new town of Hays City by 1867. Since going by railway cut off many days of travel, people wishing to go to Santa Fe used the train with greater frequency until that part of the Santa Fe Trail east of Cottonwood Creek, including the Narrows, Council Grove, and Diamond Springs, was abandoned. The trail "began to bend like a vine toward this stouter trunk [Hays City], and to wither at the roots," lamented Duffus, and in the progress of this steel-shafted penetration of the west, greater segments of the trail were abandoned.

In the winter of 1868 the Atcheson and Topeka Railroad began its trek across Kansas. Beginning at Topeka, the A&T tracks were laid westward at an amazing rate, and five years later reached La Junta, Colorado. In many places paralleling the route of the old trail, this line gave birth to Dodge City, which quickly took over the functions of Santa Fe.

Born in an exciting and turbulent era, Dodge City became the terminus of great Texas cattle drives. Here, buyers would purchase trail-hardened cattle and ship them over the rails to Chicago for processing. The drovers were paid off in Dodge City, and found many outlets for the pent-up emotions caused by the boredom of driving thousands of lowing brutes to market. In addition to the legitimate merchants, gamblers, con men and prostitutes were more than eager to relieve the cowpunchers of their newly-acquired riches. Too, since Dodge City was the main settlement along the new route west, determined settlers and greasy buffalo hunters added to its teeming, boisterous throngs, while commerce in Santa Fe continued to shrink.

On account of Santa Fe's commercial decline and its relatively inaccessible location, the Atcheson and Topeka route west bypassed this once-thriving community. New track laying techniques were developed, though, and this, coupled with political pressure, caused the railroad to extend a branch line northward from Lamy to Santa Fe.

Progress was slow, but determined crews labored mightily, and the Sangre de Cristos echoed with the unfamiliar clang of rails being laid. Finally, the cold morning of February 9, 1880, was greeted with the chuffing of the first engine as it entered the New Mexican Territorial capital city. Shots were fired, bands played, and speeches were given in celebration of the coming of the railroad. The citizens of Santa Fe were particularly overjoyed when officials of the railroad announced its new

116

name: the Atcheson, Topeka and Santa Fe.

Caught in the celebration of happiness, priests rang mission bells, being answered in kind by that of the engine. As the bells announced the beginning of a new era for Santa Fe, they also tolled out the death knell for the Santa Fe Trail. Now sixty-one years old, the trail had served its role in the United States' growth as a nation.

There are but a few places today where hard-packed wheel ruts along the old trail route still exist. Bearing mute testimony to the vibrant history which passed their way, these tracks are being slowly eroded away by the elements and passage of time. Never again will they hear the familiar cry of "fall in," nor the chilling "Pawnee whistle." The ponderous creaking of heavily-laden wagons is now stilled, and gone is the vigorous cursing of the muleteers. All this has passed, but the very mention of the Santa Fe Trail will forever evoke proud memories about one of man's finest hours, the winning of the West.

Melvin C. Warren

117

The Dodge City Trail
by **DEAN KRAKEL**

Illustrations by:
Melvin C. Warren

Melvin C. Warren 1963

THE HISTORY of the great cattle trail up
from Texas to Dodge City and the story of
Dodge itself is forever engrained into the
fabric of the American West. Few epochs have been as factually researched or thoroughly
fictionalized and dramatically distorted as has that of the cattle drive days of Dodge City.

The men who really made the town one of
the hell raising meccas of the old West were the cattle drovers who came up the Dodge
City Trail. In the minds of millions of Americans today, principally through the medium
of television, things still happen there. The Texas herds are still pouring into Dodge City's
shipping pens, the piano player at the Long Branch continues to bang away at ivory keys
and some lean gentlemanly appearing Marshall strolls about Dodge streets.

The Dodge City Trail, some 600 miles in
length, give or take a week's walking, is unique in a historical sense in that it was to
become identified as being a part of the great Western Trail. In the first years of usage

when a high percentage of the herds were going to market in Dodge, the trail was identified as such; if, however, the herds had another destination such as the Dakotas, Wyoming or Montana, then the identification was usually, "up the Western Trail."

Each trail, the Chisholm, Western, Dodge City, Chisum, or Goodnight-Loving, had its own geographical peculiarities, favorable points as well as hazards; yet in spite of individual characteristics of each trail, tough minded cattle owners and their drovers appreciated the fact that a straight line was usually the shortest distance between two points.

The trail to Dodge City had its beginning in March of 1866. A new adventure was underway in the sleepy little town of San Antonio. During the years of the Civil War cattle had been multiplying on the ranges of Texas. By the time the War was over more than 5,000,000 wild cattle were feeding on Texas' broad ranges; with beef commanding high prices in the North and East, there was quick acceptance of the idea that herds be driven north by buyers who had already purchased them for city markets.

And so, in the spring of the second year of peace following the Civil War herds totaling about 250,000 head were gathered in and about San Antonio. The long drive began up the trail known as the Shawnee Trail, which ran West of Fort Worth, then crossing the Red River into Indian Territory passing Fort Gibson, and a somewhat hazardous drive to Baxter Springs in southeastern Kansas.

The pushing of the herds of Longhorns north during this first year proved to be disastrous for a number of reasons. A contributing factor was the lack of experience on the part of the drovers. River crossings, attacks and thievery on the part of both white and red men caused heavy losses. Upon reaching the borders of Kansas and Missouri; trail bosses were met by angered settlers who feared the spread of the dreaded Texas fever to their own stock, which had caused heavy losses in earlier years.

Many owners, in the face of losses and difficulties, sold their herds before reaching the end of drives and returned to Texas. Those who were successful in reaching Baxter Springs or other points along the railroad, arrived with herds greatly reduced in both numbers and weight. The cost of making the drive, losses, and freight charges to the point at which owners found buyers, added up to discouragement. The following year saw few Texas herds on the Shawnee Trail.

In the meantime another plan was underway. In Kansas the railroad was building westward from Kansas City up the valley of the Kaw River and Joseph G. McCoy, a shrewd cattle buyer from Springfield, Illinois, decided to establish facilities for reception and purchase of Texas cattle somewhere along the line. He chose the little town of Abilene in a virtually unsettled region 170 miles West of Kansas City. The area surrounding the site chosen by McCoy, was flat grassland with an ample supply of water. McCoy had shipping pens, barns, stables and a hotel built, and advertised his plans widely. The end of the summer of 1867 was one of marked success with more than 35,000 head arriving, but it was only the beginning of one of history's greatest exoduses.

Abilene brought into being the Chisholm Trail. The new road was named in honor of Jessie Chisholm, a half breed Indian cowman and trader who was first to drive over its lower reaches, avoiding the difficult obstacles of the former trail. The Chisholm Trail ran from the vicinity of San Antonio to the Red River, into Indian Territory to Fort Reno, passing through where the towns of Caldwell, Wichita, and Newton were to be, on the Abilene. But Abilene was not destined to remain the chief cowtown of Kansas. In 1871, the Santa Fe Railroad, competing with the Kansas Pacific reached Newton, Kansas, and a year later was extended through and beyond Dodge City.

It was Dodge City that was to become the queen of the cowtowns; a crown she was to wear undisputed for more than a decade. The significant factor in Dodge's importance was the use of the great Western Trail by cattlemen in searching for markets for their herds. The Dodge City Trail began in the vicinity of Austin, Texas, ran north past Fort Griffin near the Brazos River to the Red River, crossing that unpredictable body of water to Doan's famous store, into Greer County through Indian held lands, principally of the Kiowa-Comanche and Cheyenne-Arapaho, then on to the Cherokee outlet and into Kansas crossing the Arkansas west of Dodge City. Significantly, this destination for some was the "half way point" as herds moved on to northern shipping points along the Union Pacific Railroad, such as the one at Ogallala in Nebrasha. Others were sold to the government and delivered to Indian Agencies at Pine Ridge, Rosebud and Standing Rock; herds were often driven to Colorado, Wyoming, or Montana. It was through the Dodge City corridor that millions of beeves were moved. In a sense, Dodge City as a shipping point became the stockyards of America; and from this point a large percentage of the high plains east of the Rockies was to gain its stock.

From 1869 to 1884 was the golden age of the Trails as it was for the cattle industry of the open range. Estimates indicate that during this period more than 7.5 million head of Texas cattle went north. Manuscript records indicate that during six weeks early in the summer of 1880, fifty seven herds, totaling upward of 125,000 head passed various points enroute to Dodge city. Certainly this year was not considered the high tide in driving herds north. In fact, it was a period of decline.

The rules and practices on the Dodge City Trail were fixed in a code of its own. The stock was given a road brand and the first days out were usually slow and filled with adjustments. Once the herd was trail broken, fifteen miles a day, or about three hundred per month, was usually considered good time. If care were exercised a herd could gain weight on the drive.

Experience taught cattlemen that 2,500 head

was a practical number to move. The handling of such a herd usually called for a dozen men, with fifty to seventy horses, and a chuck wagon which was often drawn by mules.

Trail cowboys were usually paid from $25.00 to $40.00 and trail bosses from $100.00 to $150.00 per month. If there were no losses or mishaps on the way, it cost about $1,500.00 and three months of time to drive an average size herd from Bandera to Dodge City, or about sixty cents a head for the trip. Horses were usually supplied by the owner of the cattle, but each cowboy furnished his own saddle and bedroll. At the end of the drive it was the custom to sell all of the horses except one for each of the men returning to Texas. It was also a common practice of drovers owning ranches on northern ranges to dispatch remudas of horses from their holdings in the north to meet the drovers at Dodge City, or some point on the trail, and the Texas horses would be sent back to ranches.

It was the custom of the trail outfits to break camp after a predawn breakfast; and to permit the cattle to move slowly away from bedding ground, grazing as they went during the first hours of the day. When in this manner the herd had become well strung out—a herd of 2,500 head was usually five miles long from head to drag—a quickened pace was taken and maintained until the noon hour. Meanwhile the cook had pushed a few miles ahead of the herd with his chuck wagon, and at some suitable place had made camp in which to prepare the meal. During and after this midday meal the herd rested a couple of hours, then the drive was resumed. The cook again pushed ahead with the chuck wagon to make camp for the night at some point selected by the trail boss.

Two or three old and experienced cowboys usually rode at the head of a herd to direct its movements, prevent possbile mixups with other herds, and check threatened stampedes. The younger men had the task of keeping the herd together and giving special attention to the lame, stubborn, or sick critters. Often drovers following cattle or at their flanks were in clouds of dust for long periods of time. A wrangler with extra horses was sometimes in advance of the herd or trailing beside it. The trail Boss could always be found at the place where he was most needed at the moment; usually he was riding ahead to confer with other point riders and to note the condition of grass and watering sites.

Uniquely the trail to Dodge City had its own chronicles; in the many songs and ballads composed enroute by cowboys. These songs have helped to keep alive the colorful legends of the cattle trails. Few ballads record as factually as does "John Garner's Trail Herd."

This tune starts off with, "Listen to my song, I'll relate to you about the time you remember well, when we, with old John Garner, drove a beef herd up the trail." The writer tells that the work started early in the spring and preparations were under way. The outfit was a good one, good men, good horses. "Through and through—it was a jolly crew."

126

The size of the herd was given as two thousand or more. Then the writer takes eight lines to tell of the problems the outfit had in getting the herd lined out or trail broken. They were "wild beeves as you ever saw," and they literally hung onto them by the tail, closing out the two stanzas with, "Oh, you know we had a circus as we all went up the trail. The cattle tried to turn back and every night they stampeded—without fail."

Whoever wrote or sung about a drive seldom fails to mention the crises created by crossing the Red River, leaving Texas, entering Indian Territory, or Oklahoma. The problem of the inspector at the river is not passed over lightly by the composer. If he, the inspector, did harm to old John, the boss, the outfit would get his scalp on down the trail—a purely western understanding. The outfit was uneasy when on the Indian Reservation, but the men knew old John Garner was tough as hell, tried and true—"That old bald headed cow thief would surely take us through." The composer then hits Dodge City hard and affording the opportunity to sing out:

When we reached Dodge we drew our four months pay,

Times were better then, boys, that was a better day.

The way we drank and gambled and threw the girls around

Say, a crowd of Texas cowboys has come to take our town.

The elemental facts of the drive north over the trail to Dodge City are contained in this wonderful old ballad, as well as the philosophy of the hired men who worked as drovers. For the cowhand there were both hardship and fun—the kind that has to be experienced and is almost impossible to relate. In summing it up the composer sings, "The cowboy's life is a dreary life, though his mind, it is no load, and he always spends his money like he found it in the road."

Some of America's foremost historians and writers have recorded the adventures of the Dodge City Trail. None of the accounts however, are more important or significant to me than those written by men who actually made the drive.

A classic narrative of cowboy life and trail driving facts is *We Pointed Them North* by E. C. Abbott. Abbott's account sparkles with frankness and is pungent as the smell of mud at the Red River crossing. The drive Abbott experienced took place a long time after the guess work had gone out of the trail routing, but the drive covered the full length from Texas to Miles City. It was "a helluva long way," wrote cowboy artist C. M. Russell, "no matter how you looked at it."

Frank Collinson in *Life In the Saddle*, gives a full description of a drive up the trail to Dodge in 1873. Hired by Texas cattleman, John T. Lytle, and his cousin, Tom McDaniel, the outfit's plan was to drive 3,500 head of "good, big, aged, steers to the Red Cloud Agency, delivering them not later than August 1, the following year."

Lytle ranched in the southeastern corner of Medina County, Texas, running his stock on the open range and also fencing several thousand acres. Collinson's accounts are good in detail. In describing the formation of the herd, he wrote, "It was a mesquite brush country, but the grass was good and water plentiful. There were cattle all over the country from the Rio Grande on the West, and to the Gulf Coast on the east. Many ranchmen were rounding up and trail driving cattle both to Kansas and California."

The outfit left Lytle's Ranch for the trail March 16, 1874. There were eighteen men, some of whom Collinson says were veteran trail hands, and a horse remuda of around one hundred head. "Our mess wagon," Collinson said, "was pulled by four good horses. Our bedding was carried in this wagon, which Lytle had laid the law down about overloading. He said the roads would be rough and if the wagon was too heavy the horses could not keep up with the steers. As a consequence our bedding was rather thin—one pair of blankets and a wagon sheet to each man. We slept two in a bed and doubled our supplies. We were comfortable enough, unless it rained and our bed got soaked, which was often the case."

Collinson says the greatest trouble with the herd was stampeding. In talking about the trail he recalled that since we planned to head across unknown country, apparently deviating from the established route in search of grass, from Fort Griffin, Texas, to Camp Supply, Indian Territory, the army furnished Lytle with a guide, who well knew the country, the watering places, etc.

From Supply to Fort Dodge the trail was plainly marked according to Collinson. Grass and water were fine in the Arkansas Valley near Dodge and it was here, too, that several of the boys saw their first train. Lytle rode ahead to examine the river and found it fordable. "We planned to cross over the next day. This would be the first time the herd would have to swim." Frank Collinson makes little mention of Dodge City, even though he spent two days there. He called it a typically "western ragtown. . . ."

Bob Fudge went to work for a Texas cattleman, Ab Blocker, in 1882, and started north with two thousand grown cattle. Fudge's account of the Western Trail to Dodge and onto the Little Bighorn country is revealing.

"I have heard people say a cowboy had nothing on his mind but his hat," Fudge wrote. "Well, those cattle were never left alone for one minute in four months, night or day, without two to four cowboys near them. Maybe we didn't have anything on our minds but a stetson hat—but we had a mighty responsibility hung on us somewhere."

"At night the cattle were herded, going on the bed ground a little after sundown, when three men were left with them, riding in a circle around them, pushing any steer or cow back into the herd that started to graze or walk out from the sleeping, grunting, mass, inside our 'circle.'

"We had, during the night, four guards: first, second, third, and fourth. These separate guards were on for two hours each. When the two hours were up one of the trio would go into camp and call the next guard. The last guards also called the cook, at an appointed hour which was very early, generally before daylight.

"This 'standing guard,' as night herding was called, was the hardest part of a cowboy's life. Of course, we got used to getting up at our appointed time but when the weather was bad, as in a rain or sleet storm, a poor cowhand shivered all through his guard, in cold wet clothes, and perhaps kept shivering until the sun came out the next morning, or maybe several days later when the weather cleared.

"Sometimes during a storm we were all with the cattle during the entire night, and sometimes part hearded until midnight when the other half were called from their nervous slumbers to "hold" the herd until daylight.

"We had special horses for night guard which we called our night horse. We picked a gentle horse and one that was well stake-broke. We staked our night horses close to camp where we could mount at a minute's notice. These horses were also saddled before being staked. We each had a rope used for this purpose and a stake, generally a wooden pin, which we drove into the ground. In this way every man had a horse handy anytime during the night.

"As we travelled north day after day, when the weather was fine there wasn't a man in our outfit that would have traded places with a king. There was game everywhere in northern Texas. In the early mornings wild turkeys and deer were almost always in our vision."

Fudge tells about an interesting incident on the trail concerning Indians and the fortitude of the trail boss.

"The Boss had us corral the horses in our rope corral fastened to the wagon. He told us that it was "every man for himself and the Devil for us all." We threw our bedrolls on the ground and everything that we thought would stop a bullet or an arrow or protect even a part of our bodies. We did not have to wait long for the Indians to come in sight again. They were travelling at about the same pace as when they first approached us. There wasn't much said between our little outfit until now; all but one man who refused to do a thing but lie in the bottom of the wagon and hide like a lizard had been preparing to make our last stand. Now, we commenced talking.

129

It was sort of a relief that the Indians were coming in daylight.

"When the Chief got within about one hundred yards of us he stopped his outfit and raised a white flag on a stick which was to show us he had accepted our terms. The Chief got off his horse and pawed the dust. I don't know why he did this unless it was to get the sort of dust he wanted for he took a handful of this dust and threw it in the air. I can still see that dust; it seemed to go clear up to the sky. This was to show the other Indians that they would come peaceably to the feast, I reckon. We all wondered why he had spared our lives. We would find out the next day.

"We strung our herd north again and the boss cut out about twenty head of foot sore and crippled cattle and the Indians accepted them without even a grunt. The Indians commenced butchering those cattle as soon as they were in their possession. We moved on several miles further and bedded our herd for the night. Every precaution was taken. The guard was doubled and the horse wrangler was told to stay with the horses. We did not fear the Indians we had made the deal with (as their hides were filled with beef) as much as the thoughts that there might be a thousand more Indians in these Wichita Mountains which was a great hangout for the Comanches."

James C. Shaw went up the Dodge City Trail in 1879. The herd was formed up in the vicinity of Belton, Texas, north of Austin. The route was a well worn road but nonetheless filled with peril and risk. Shaw's account of life around Fort Griffin, Texas, is important. In signing on with Dick Withers, Shaw agreed to wages of $40.00 a month and use of his three horses. Shaw wrote his memoirs, which were published under the title, *North From Texas*. He recalled the work of the cowboys as being difficult since 1,800 of the almost 5,000 head in the herd were yearlings from the coastal country of Texas. Shaw tells of the outfit moving north to Dodge City. "We struck the trail running from Fort Worth to Fort Dodge, Kansas, and along this trail there were many carcasses of horses and old work oxen."

In crossing into Indian Territory Shaw said, "The next river was the Red River and when we got to it, it looked a mile wide, but it was not swimming deep except for a short distance. There were three channels that were swimming; but when I reached the river the cattle were going in nicely and the only trouble we had was when some of the cattle bogged and we had to pull them out."

The account of coming into Kansas is interesting. "We had all kinds of trouble with the new settlers. They would plow a furrow and if we crossed over they would have us pulled and fined and under no consideration would they allow us to cross unless it was time to bed the cattle and they would give us all kinds of inducements to camp on their land, so they could use the Buffalo chips for fuel next winter. They would guard them like a Texas man does a watermelon patch, until they were ripe enough to haul in."

Shaw thought little of Dodge City. He went into the town to go to a general store. Though there only a short while, he saw a woman who had apparently been hit in the face with a pistol, concluding, "I was anxious to get out of Dodge City."

"Suply I T
Jun 10, 1887

Deer Brouthr Erwin

It has been somtim sincist i writ you We hav cum lon way sinc. We bout los or selvs in tha river. Tim is gud an porly. We leav 1 or bys in a cole grav. We los about 1/10 the criters tha bos say most a cont themb red Debils, who watced usns like cyote du the hon dogs. Sum tak, oter stel or we giv thm lam cows the et lik hogs gutz en al. then tha beet daun un holw al nit. tha hurd is techy wez sick. if'n i neber see a injine wit or witou hisun pant face i be hapy. tha lord had nuthin ta do wit thm dirte devils ben on his arth. Prays hem. Sum cow men cum into or camp, goin to Banda. Thy ben ta Dodg i guesst. it mus be a hell hol i belivid. Me dont giv a tot, boy a purty face wood lok gud ta ths sun of Tenisee. Shor wood lik ta se a trm ankl and sinc ma toofs in a woma bak cak and fil ma bely wih somthen tha lik of or chuc bux ant seed. 2 or bys says tha ant goin to Mountan. if Mr. Chalk wans i'l be wit him as i wood ma oun dady. i wil sav ma nicke an try ma chanst up ther. i hopes yu ar fin brouthr. giv ma luv ta or deer sistars. writ me if you wood bu i not sur whn i cath it.

Yours oblig brouthr
Will Porter"

The Porter letter, heretofore unpublished, is one of six letters that make up this unusual but nonetheless important account. Will Porter worked for E. S. Newman, whose extensive ranching operations were in northern Nebraska and later in Eastern Montana. There are several references in standard histories to Newman's cattle raising activities as well as his banking interests in Nebraska and Montana. The Porter letters written to his brother, Erwin, in Memphis, Tennessee, are of the trail driving days classics, although the degree of illegibility detracts from their charm. The letters bear post marks of Fort Worth, Texas; Camp Supply, Indian Territory; Dodge City, Kansas; Ogallala, Nebraska; Fort Laramie, Wyoming Territory; and Miles City, Montana. The final letter in the collection is filled with both anticipation and excitement; at last he would get to see Miles City—the end of his rainbow and do all the things that he had dreamed of doing during those hard months on the trail.

Research has not turned up a Will Porter clue.

The newspapers' files in Miles City reveal nothing of him nor do the libraries in Tennessee. If the trail herd account books of E. H. Newman are extant, no doubt they will contain mention of Porter.

In his last letter, Porter writes of plans for coming home. His experiences in Texas on the Dodge City Trail, and into Nebraska and the northern plains no doubt taught him much; perhaps he had reappraised life's values, and was determined to become a better man, as he wrote, "I by mi a nu sadle wiht tha stars of Texs on it, an cumb hume prud wiht silvr in tha bag."

The Goodnight-Loving Trail
by **DONALD BUBAR**

Illustrations by:
Melvin C. Warren

Melvin C. Warren

THE END of civil war found Texas prostrate, in ruin, collasped by total defeat. Confederate money was worthless. Trade stagnated. People were destitute. In many areas local government was non-existent. The string of frontier forts built and manned by United States troops in the 1840s and '50s, under whose protection the Texas frontier had moved rapidly westward, was abandoned by the Federal Government with the advent of war in 1861.

During the war years the state lacked the power to man the forts and to defend adequately the frontier citizens from the ravages of the Indians. The tribes had nominally been assigned reservations in Indian Territory and New Mexico, and indeed one Comanche clan was allotted a reservation on the upper Brazos. But, unguarded save by the paper-thin forces of the Texas Frontier Regiment, the Indians roamed central Texas almost at will, killing, kidnapping, burning and looting. At war's end four-fifths of all frontier ranches had been abandoned. In some counties not a white settler remained.

The returning soldier was apt to find his family penniless and in rags, driven from their land—his cottage burned, his farm in weeds, his livestock stolen. To compound his miseries, 1866 was a drought year. The economic resources of Texas had been drained away and dissipated. There were critical shortages everywhere. Almost everywhere, that is.

One and only one commodity glutted the market in Texas. That was cattle, Texas cattle as they were then called, but which we now know as the Longhorn. During the war years herds had roamed free along the frontier range and their numbers had multiplied into the millions. Unbranded and undomesticated, they were claimed by the first taker who could get his mark on them. And though these Longhorns were half wild, they could be trailed. Here was a commodity in super-abundance, looking for a market.

Gold is where you find it. George Jackson broke the ice on Chicago Creek in Colorado on a bitter January afternoon in 1859. With his hunting knife he chopped loose enough sand from the stream-bed to pan out nine dollars in gold in an hour. Marking the spot well, he returned to the village of Denver to await spring.

The announcement of his and of John Gregory's later find that year in Gregory Gulch triggered off a stampede to timberline in the Colorado Rockies. The Civil War retarded this drive but at the end of the strife it was rekindled with zeal and determination. Men from both North and South who had acquired the self-discipline to endure hardship on a hundred battlefields hurled themselves against the eastern face of the Rockies with impetuous resolve. Each gulch was examined and cross-examined. The sand and gravel of a thousand streams were subjected to an inquisition. Granite cliffs were compelled to yield their secret hoards to the insatiable lust of the hard rock miners.

Towns sprang up with each fresh gold or silver strike. Gregory's discovery claim was at the geographical center of what for decades was rightly known as "the richest square mile on earth". Within eight years the virgin mountain glen was teeming with the ten thousand inhabitatants of Central City and its satellite towns. Elsewhere along the front range it was the same. Denver was the booming metropolis which undergirt the mining industry throughout the Rockies.

Mining is hard work and miners must be well-fed. But no farming or ranching industry existed in Colorado to support the boom. Dairy produce and other perishable foodstuffs were scarce in Denver and out of the question in the mountains. Staples such as flour and corn meal, dried beans and dried fruits, salt pork, sorghum and coffee, were freighted in by wagon from the slowly advancing railhead. The miner supplemented this diet with venison, elk and bear meat occasionally; and he fought off scurvy with wild onions, dandelion salad and rose hip tea. He did not know why he drank this tea, but seventy-five years later it was discovered that wild mountain rose hips contain the highest concentrate of vitamin C found in nature.

But the miner needed beef in his diet, and this was an almost unobtainable luxury. Lack of refrigeration made it impossible to freight in fresh meat. The buffalo was too wild and intractible to round up on trail. If beef was to be imported, it had to furnish its own transportation and come on the hoof. Once there, it commanded fancy prices. An adult steer frequently brought $80.00 or more in Denver, and as high as $120.00 back in the hills. And so this area was a seller's market, the best east of the Rockies.

The incentive behind all Texas cattle drives of the '60s and '70s is implicit in the Department of Agriculture statistics of the cattle prices in the northern states. The 1867 figures for 3-year old steers were:

Missouri	$32.83
Kansas	38.40
Illinois	40.19
New Jersey	70.58
New York	68.57
Massachusetts	86.00

The Department reported the average price of 3-year old steers in Texas in 1867 at $9.46. It estimated the total number of Texas cattle that year at 3,111,475. This guess was wilder than the cattle themselves. All informed cattlemen agreed it was far too low. At the war's end, mature cattle on local Texas markets brought $3.00 to $4.00 a head and fat beeves $5.00 to $6.00. They were offered frequently along the range at $1.00 to $2.00 per head, with few takers.

Texas was not lacking in the men willing to take the gamble and endure the hardships and dangers of a cattle drive. Many famous Texas ranches were started from the profits made during the '60s and '70s on drives to the northern and eastern markets. But among them all, in breadth of imagination, in sound business judgment, in fortitude and courage, in wise leadership, in knowledge of the western frontier, none surpassed Oliver Loving and Charles Goodnight, who as partners blazed the original trail which bore their names.

Charles Goodnight was born in Illinois the day before the fall of the Alamo. At the age of nine his family moved to Milam County, Texas. Charles rode the distance astride a young mare, bareback. At 21 he moved to Palo Pinto County and became a ranger, Indian scout and guide for a frontier regiment during the Civil War. In 1865 he gathered a herd and ranged them in the fertile Keechi Valley in Palo Pinto and Jack Counties, intent upon trailing them to the best available market. Now 29 years of age, inured to hardship, steeped in the geography of the western frontier, skilled in the ways of the wily Indian, possessing a consummate knowledge of Texas cattle and cow ponies, endowed with an unerring sense of direction and a passion for detailed planning, Charles Goodnight was perfectly fitted to conceive and execute the ingenious plan to capture the Colorado beef market. And Goodnight had a partner quite as remarkable as he: Oliver Loving.

Loving migrated to Texas with his family from Kentucky in 1845, at the age of 33. He was a successful cattle trader, farmer, merchant and freighter. He acquired large herds of Longhorns which for a less crowded range he moved from Collin to Palo Pinto County in 1855. One of the early drives was that made by Oliver Loving in 1858 when he trailed a herd from Palo Pinto County to Chicago by the Shawnee Trail. In 1860 he blazed a trail to Denver to cash in on the gold rush, driving north to the Arkansas River and upstream to Pueblo. Wintering here, he drove north to Denver in the spring of 1861. During the Civil War he helped to provision Confederate armies with Texas beef by trailing beef from Palo Pinto County across the Mississippi. Loving, who was Goodnight's senior by 24 years, brought to the partnership proven business acumen and a sound knowledge of the cattle industry. But the quality possessed by both men, which sealed the partnership into a union which survived death, was unquestioned personal integrity. The one indispensable ingredient which made the winning of the west possible was the sure knowledge that every man would come to his neighbor's aid, at any time, at any risk, and at any sacrifice. This spirit of mutual aid pervaded Goodnight's and Loving's outfit from the start, and gave it an *esprit de corps*which stood fast against every hardship and misfortune.

In 1865 Charles Goodnight had gathered 2000 head with the intention of driving them to New Mexico and Colorado. They had been moved to a range on Elm Creek west of the Brazos in Throckmorton County when the Indians stampeded the herd and drove it off. Not to be thwarted, he made plans anew for the following year. In fact at this time Goodnight had planned to leave Texas for good and settle in New Mexico or Colorado. Between reconstruction woes, thieving neighbors, drought, and lack of protection from the Indians, it seemed wisest to pull up stakes and move.

While making his preparations, Goodnight chanced to visit with Loving, who was also gathering and holding a herd north of Weatherford for a drive. The two compared notes, discussed objectives, weighed hazards. Then they found themselves in complete agreement. The fruition of their plan was the original trail known as the Goodnight and Loving Trail.

When on the morning of the sixth day of the sixth month of the year 1866, Loving and Goodnight broke camp in southeastern Throckmorton County and set forth with a herd of two thousand Longhorns and an outfit of eighteen men, headed for New Mexico and Colorado, they had no sense of historical mission. They had a practical desire to make money and the fortitude to take the risks. The Longhorn has now disappeared, as has his distant kinsman, the buffalo. The open range itself has forevermore been subjugated by barbed wire. The Indians waste away in enforced idleness on their reservations. But so long as man's pulse quickens to tales of courageous resolve, their accomplishments will go echoing down through the corridors of time.

Theirs was indeed a strange trail to take for those intent upon reaching Denver. Had they been headed for Mexico City or California it would have been more understandable. Southwest lay the course for hundreds of miles. Elsewhere in this book will be found the absorbing story of the Butterfield Overland Stage route across Texas, established in 1857 and maintained until Civil War brought it to a halt in 1861. Now the stations and forts which had serviced and defended this mail line were abandoned and in decay. But the route had been chosen as affording the best terrain and water. This was the route Loving and Goodnight decided to take as far as the Pecos River. Passing the remains of Camp Cooper, they crossed the Clear Fork of the Brazos at the last settlement outpost, where in the following year Fort Griffin would be established. The trail then wound through Antelope Hills and on past the spectral remains of Fort Phantom Hill, also situated on the Clear Fork. The track now veered almost due south for forty miles, passing near the present Tye, Texas, on through Buffalo Gap in the Callahan Divide in Taylor County. From here the route carried them to Fort Chadbourne in Coke County, which had only recently been re-occupied by a detachment of Federal troops after a five year abandonment during the Civil War. Next the herd was driven southwesterly to a ford in the Colorado River near the present town of Robert Lee, then over the North Concho, and on to the Middle Concho. It then turned due west as it followed up this watercourse until the stream at last petered out in the breaks of the Llano Estacado, becoming Centralia Draw.

While the herd and the horses are being rested and permitted to drink their fill from the last pools on the Middle Concho in preparation for the tortures of the "dry drive" to the Pecos, we shall pause to consider the route they have taken and the reasons for it. Goodnight and Loving have trailed their cattle over 220 miles from their home range and are now farther from Denver than when they left. They have in fact reached a point 135 miles farther south than the one from which they started. They described this path as "taking roundance." But it assuredly was the safest.

Loving, as we earlier learned, trailed the first cattle to Denver in 1858 by way of Kansas and along the Arkansas River. This route also was much longer than the direct path through the Texas Panhandle. Goodnight had become completely familiar with the eastern Staked Plains region during his four years as scout and Indian fighter with the Texas Frontier regiment. Both knew the shorter route through the Texas Panhandle was out of the question. It would have carried them straight into the heart of the Comanche and Kiowa country, whose various tribes made their homes in villages along the Canadian River. The area from Palo Duro Canyon north beyond the Canadian was strictly unknown territory for all except the Plains Indians and those New Mexico cattle thieves who traded with them. A company of cavalry as escort would hardly have sufficed to protect the herd.

The final choice between the route through Kansas and the trail through New Mexico rested upon pure business considerations; two potential markets were better than one. The pent-up demand from the miners in the Rockies was well known. But Loving and Goodnight drew some very shrewd conclusions from the Federal Government's Indian policy. The government was committed to keep all of the Indians upon their reservations. This cut the Apaches and Navajos off from their main source of food—the buffalo—which ranged to the east of the Pecos. Accordingly the U.S. Government signed a treaty with the Navajos and Utes to supply them with beef for immediate consumption, as well as seed cattle to build herds. Where was there a source of supply to satisfy these requirements? Nowhere but the Texas cattle country 400 miles to the East. These beef purchases were to be made through the army commissary at Fort Sumner on the Pecos. If the price at Fort Sumner were acceptable, Denver would have to wait.

Goodnight's and Loving's roundabout trail almost doubled the distance to Denver for drovers from North Central Texas. But the route they pioneered was made to order for cattlemen from South Texas. As we shall see, a substantial share of all cattle driven to market followed their lead until in the fullness of time barbed wire and the railroad forever put an end to these migrations.

Returning now to that wild and desolate area of West Texas at the southern extremity of the Great Plains, a land of mesquite and greasewood, prickly pear and prairie dog, coyote and rattlesnake, we find Goodnight and Loving ready to cast the die in the most critical gamble of their careers. When the possibilities of this route were first discussed by them, Loving had expressed grave misgivings about this waterless stretch between the Middle Concho and the Pecos. When the Butterfield Overland Mail Route had been laid out nineteen years before, special provision had been made for water in this wasteland. Tanks had been dug at intervals to hold stock water hauled in barrels by freighter from the Pecos and the Concho. At the risk of intruding upon the exciting story of the Butterfield Overland Mail, we quote this extract from the diary of a passenger who had made the trip in 1859, for it so dramatically highlights the immediate and pressing danger:

> October 1. . . . At dark, with fresh strong team and additional rifles and revolvers on board, we entered upon that old terror of immigrants, the Great Staked Plains. In the cold, dreary night this barren table land stretched far—an utter sand waste with a few shrubs of cactus and grease-wood. A few weeks before, travellers had narrowly escaped death from thirst. At one stage-station, during four-fifths of the year water for the mules was hauled in casks twenty-two miles

October 2. Daylight found us on a shoreless ocean of desolation. Excepting the faint mail road,

"Nor dint of hoof nor print of foot
Lay in the wild and arid soil;
No sign of travel, none of toil—
The very air was mute."

The ancient Mexicans marked a route with stakes over this vast desert, and hence its name. . . . We journeyed for eighty miles across a corner of the desert, passing two or three mail stations, the most desolate and lonely of human habitations. Then through a winding canyon we descended into the broad valley of Pecos River.

The stage line had long since been abandoned. The eroded tanks lie parched with alkali dust. The way-stations, toppled in ruinous decay, stood as portents of death and disaster for any man so foolhardy as to pit flesh and blood against the inexorable malevolence of the heat-hazed desert.

Late in the afternoon, when the cattle had taken on all the water they would accept, and with every barrel and canteen filled, the outfit struggled slowly up Centralia Draw. The next day, without water, they debouched out onto the plain, and in a cloud of bitter alkali dust drifting slowly westward, plodded on under the baleful glare of an unforgiving sun. When night brought neither water nor cooling relief from thirst and it was found that the herd could not be bedded down, the decision was made to press on by day and by night without rest or sleep for either man or beast. The weak cattle dropped in their tracks and died. Some, going blind, staggered aimlessly away from the herd and were abandoned. Others, crazed and wild, were driven off. The incomparable cow ponies, burdened with their riders and pressed without respite to keep the herd moving and confined to the trail, suffered in patient silence, while the hoarse shouts of the men were barely audible above the din of the brawling herd. Ahead of the pointers rode Goodnight, to pick out the trail through darkest night, to maintain a lookout for Indians, to search for any possible oasis in this desert. Behind rode Loving, the conservator, whose self-imposed duty it was to round up and urge back into the herd every lowly drag which could be kept to the trail. Twice the age of most of the men in the outfit, Loving drove himself almost to the limit of human endurance to save the expedition from financial disaster. Between these two, and as staunch and uncomplaining as either leader, struggled the eighteen hired hands of the outfit. Among these were some whose names would embellish the ranching annals of Texas for decades to come.

On the morning of the fourth day the suffering herd wound down through Castle Gap. At a distance of several miles they detected the scent of water, and becoming unmanageable, they stampeded down to the Pecos at Horsehead Crossing. Water and grass—but above all, water. At a cost of 300 head, Goodnight and Loving had won. What they learned here would make every future passage through this desert easier.

We will rejoin the outfit later, as it breaks the trail up the Pecos, but now is the time for us to get acquainted with the economic and technical aspects of a cattle drive.

It would be found by experience that in trailing a herd to market, about 2,500 head was the optimum number. Fifty percent of all cattle trailed to market were in herds of from 2,000 to 3,000. It required almost as many men to handle the lesser number as the greater; but more than 3,000 was likely to prove troublesome.

Frequently a drive would be a joint undertaking by several cattlemen, and each of them might have acquired cattle with wide diversity of origin. In consequence it was customary to trail-brand the cattle before departure for ease of identification and segregation along the route and at the end of the trail.

Normally cattle would pick up weight on the trail if the drive was unhurried and with ample water and grass accessible. About ten to fifteen miles a day would be an average advance, depending upon weather, terrain, composition of the herd. Many drivers would not trail a mixed herd. Goodnight's and Loving's first herd was steers, cows, heifers and calves, but Goodnight says that never again did he take a mixed herd on this trail, though he did on others. If the herd were beef headed for the slaughter pens, it was more likely to consist of steers. But where some cattle might be sold to stock the range, mixed herds predominated.

An average herd required about twelve men to work it. During the sixties and early seventies the number of men ran higher because of danger from Indians, but after the latter were locked up tightly on the reservations, the number lessened. Each cowboy required from six to eight horses. Thus a remuda of ponies would consist of a hundred head or more in charge of the wrangler.

The operating cost of a herd on the trail was from $500 to $600 per month—perhaps even higher on the Goodnight Trail. Thus it cost from 60 cents to a dollar a head to trail a steer to Abilene, Kansas, or to Denver. When you consider that in the early days of trail driving, the enterprising Texas cattleman was trying to "hook a $4.00 steer up with a $40.00 market," and that his cattle would gain weight on the trail, it is apparent that the rewards for the ambitious and the daring well justified the risks.

The hazards, of course, were many; and while some were overcome as time went on, they were replaced by others which if not more dangerous, were certainly more exasperating. Without describing, we mention some of these: unstable market prices, Indians, drought, floods, disease, stampedes, prairie fires, wild animals, blizzards, barbed wire, trail blockades, quarantines, branding laws, inspection laws, toll roads, and many more.

Elsewhere the physical characteristics of the peculiar breed of Texas cattle—the Longhorn—will be described. It is sufficient here to mention that they were semi-wild and had to be trail-broken. During the first weeks of a drive the cattle were difficult to control and tended to stampede without warning, particularly at night. In time they became more manageable, though the term "docile" was never apt.

Once the herd had become trail broken, the drive could be organized and routines better established. Before it had been many days on the trail, one or more natural-born leaders among the steers would assert themselves. These would be the first up on the bedding grounds and quickly move to the head of the column. Drivers would take adavantage of this natural bent for leadership. By belling the leader, the herd would become conditioned to follow the sound of the bell.

The order on the march became standard with most traildrivers. The trail boss took the head and picked the route. If the trail were a well-established one in a country where the landmarks, watercourses and natural hazards were well-known, the trail boss could fix his attention upon the pace and spacing of the herd. But in blazing a new trail a leader such as Charles Goodnight would be scouring the country as far as ten to fifteen miles ahead of the herd. His years as an army frontier scout specially prepared him for this task far beyond the abilities of most traildrivers. The first duty was to establish the route for the day, taking into account the terrain, grass and water. Deadly alkali ponds were marked and avoided. River fords were tested for quicksands. A suitable site for the night's bedding ground was selected. Signs of bad weather were noted and adjustments made accordingly. The ground was searched for Indian sign. By signal the leader learned to communicate from afar his wishes to his men.

A herd of 2,500 head on the move would extend about a mile along the trail. Off to either side of the lead steer rode a hand. These were the 'pointers' who controlled the direction of the herd and the pace. About a third of the way back were two more riders, one on either side, called the 'swing' men. They kept the cattle moving, maintaining the herd to a width of about fifty to sixty feet. A certain looseness was essential, as closely bunched cattle overheated. Tales of the heat generated by a milling herd sound incredible, but the experience was too universal to be discounted. And then, these half-wild animals trailed much better when, under easy restraint, they were left with the illusion that their movements were voluntary—guided rather than driven.

Halfway back of the 'swing' men were the 'flanks', one on either side; and at the rear were the 'dragmen', two or three in number.

These rounded up the strays and kept them moving with the herd.

The chuck wagon, driven by the cook, usually rode a short distance in advance of the herd. This conserved time. The cook could get the wagon to the bedding ground and have the evening meal under way while the herd was being rounded up and put out on the grass. By traveling in the van the cook avoided much of the dust stirred up by the sharp hooves. In the morning the dew tended to soften the hoof, and so frequently the herd would not be thrown onto the trail until the breeze had dried the grass. By this time, the cook would have cleaned up after breakfast, packed and gotten under way ahead of the herd.

The horse wrangler and his remuda would likely be also in advance of the herd, but off to the side.

If the herd were larger, more men would be required along the line. The best men in the outfit remained as pointers, but exchanged sides from day to day to equalize the amount of dust they were obliged to eat. The remaining riders would be rotated around the herd from day to day so as to balance the work load and dust. The drag men had by far the hardest task. Their ability to keep the drags moving established the pace for the herd. Their labors were unremitting.

The trail seldom ran straight. It veered to avoid broken country and badlands; it skirted timber and hills; it gave wide berth to bad waters; it sought the low passes across the mountain ranges, and the low water over the streams. It had an affinity for grass.

Let us take to the trail once more and follow Goodnight and Loving northwestward along the east bank of the Pecos, toward New Mexico. From Horsehead Crossing to Pope's Crossing, a trailing distance of a hundred and twenty-five miles, lies country which, were it not for the presence of the Pecos River winding through it, would have been one of the most forsaken, desolate and impassable areas on the continent. Every cowman whose trail experience was wide enough to afford comparison attested that this was the meanest, most God-forsaken stretch of country he had ever visited. The annual rainfall is 10 to 14 inches. The land is rolling prairie and sandhills which sustain a light cover of scrub brush and a dense population of rattlesnakes. Early travellers claimed that there were no animals or birds inhabiting this region, save only snakes and scorpions. The last stretch of desert before you reach the New Mexico line is now Loving County, named for Oliver Loving. This is a squalid memorial by which to preserve the fame of one of Texas' most courageous and distinguished frontier citizens. Loving County is so uninviting that by 1890 it had a population of only 3. It was not even organized and a county seat established until 1931. (New Mexico, which Oliver Loving looked upon as foreign soil, did better by his memory, for it named two towns, Loving and Lovington, after him.)

The water improves as you travel up the Pecos. This stream rises crystal clear and cold from the melting snows at the southern extremity of the Sangre de Cristo Range, a few miles northeast of Santa Fe. At one point near its source only 25 miles separate it from the Rio Grande. But each river takes its diverse route through the arid regions of a sub-continent, picking up sediment and alkali until, at a point south of San Angelo, hundreds of miles downstream and thousands of feet lower in elevation, this tired old Pecos, laden with silt and with salt, cuts through a deep gorge marking off the eastern boundary of Judge Roy Bean's self-declared province, and spews forth its brackish burden onto the dusty channel of the Rio Grande.

The Pecos is a river that deserves to be remembered. Coronado and his captains bridged this tumultous stream and were nourished by its limpid mountain waters in their expedition onto the Great Plains in 1540—eighty years before the Pilgrim Fathers set foot on Plymouth Rock. The Pueblo Indians established a high rise apartment village on its banks more than two hundred years before Columbus set sail for the New World. Six hundred years before the birth of Christ members of the Basketmaker clans, driven from their caves and ledges in Northern New Mexico, followed its meanderings until it brought them sanctuary in the Chisos Mountains of the Big Bend. Like all rivers, it was both a highway and a barrier. It prevented the western migration of the buffalo and served to limit the forays of the Comanche to the East and Apache to the West. The fruition of Goodnight's and Loving's dreams now require its services as a highway and as a barrier.

Instead of fording the river at Horsehead Crossing, Goodnight and Loving stayed with the east bank up to the site of Pope's Camp. In the future, however, many traildrivers preferred to ford the Pecos here and follow the west bank. Fifty-five miles upstream, at Emigrant Crossing, the trail intersected the old route from the east to California, blazed during the gold rush in the days of the Forty-Niners.

At Pope's Camp, amid the ruins of the old stage station, they crossed the Pecos and entered New Mexico. A glance at the map makes the reason for this apparent. No stream drains into the river from the sandy wastes and potash sinkholes to the east; while from the west flow numerous sparkling creeks whose headwaters are in the Guadalupe Mountains. In addition, the Pecos afforded some protection from wandering bands of Quahadi Comanches who, primarily interested in the buffalo which ranged to the east, were not likely to be found west of the river.

As the herd was trailed slowly north a new danger loomed. They were approaching Mescalero Apache country. The Apaches had been technically confined by the army, together with their traditional enemies, the Navajos, on a reservation at Fort Sumner. They broke out of the reservation a few months before and returned to their former abodes. So Goodnight and Loving crossed the Pecos once more to the east and and proceeded north along it to Fort Sumner, about 215 miles north of Horsehead Crossing.

Goodnight and Loving sold about eight

hundred head of steers to the Indian Agency at Fort Sumner for a fortune of about $40,000 in gold and bills of exchange. The Government was not interested in the cows and heifers numbering about the same. It appeared that Denver, 375 miles north as the crow flies, would prove to be the end of the trail, where another pot of gold awaited them.

A question of nomenclature intrudes just here. The cattle trail from Palo Pinto County to Denver by way of Fort Sumner is popularly known as the Goodnight Trail. Careful historians, aware that in vision, enterprise, courage and daring, Oliver Loving and Charles Goodnight shared equally in the culmination of this dream, prefer to designate the trail from Texas to Fort Sumner as the Goodnight and Loving Trail. North of Fort Sumner, as will be developed, several trails were opened. The first by Oliver Loving in 1866 is frequently called the Loving Trail. Subsequent ones into Northern Colorado and Wyoming are called the Goodnight Trail.

For several days the party continued northward along the Pecos in exuberant mood. Success had crowned their efforts; the most difficult and dangerous portion of the trail was behind them; and the work load had lightened with the diminished herd. A fresh idea had been germinating in the minds of Loving and Goodnight. While camped near the spot where Coronado, the first white man to visit these regions, erected a bridge over the Pecos three hundred and twenty-six years before, the plan was formulated. Loving would push on to Denver with the remnant of the herd. Goodnight would return home at once and immediately acquire another and get it on the trail before winter. The two would meet at Bosque Grande on the Pecos, an ideal holding spot below Fort Sumner, where grass and water were plentiful.

Goodnight and three cowboys turned back to retrace their steps toward home. Loving moved on with the remainder of the outfit. They were now in settled country, where supplies could be purchased, secure for the present from attack by plains Indians or Apaches. Loving continued up the Pecos to the village of San Miguel, striking the Santa Fe Trail where it swung around the southernmost tip of the Sangre de Cristo Range.

Following now the Santa Fe Trail, the engaging history of which is recounted elsewhere in this volume, Loving struck out over the plain to the headwaters of the Gallinas River. Passing Las Vegas, the trail veered northeastward, crossing the divide which separates the waters of the Rio Grande from those of the Mississippi, and on down into the valley of the Mora, a tributary of the Canadian. They skirted the foothills of the Turkey Mountains, crossed Ocate Creek, and moved on up the Canadian to its headwaters at Raton Pass.

The crest of the pass, by a striking coincidence, sits astride the 37th parallel of latitude marking the boundary between New Mexico and Colorado. Established by Congress in 1861, this straight boundary line is by far the longest in the United States, stretching continuously over 1,050 miles from

Missouri to Nevada as it separates Kansas, Colorado and Utah on the north from Oklahoma, New Mexico and Arizona on the south. At the summit of Raton Pass, "Uncle Dick" Wootton, one of the best publicized of the early frontiersmen, and a former Denver saloonkeeper, had set up a tollgate, claiming he had built the road over the pass. The toll was a nominal 10 cents a head, but the very idea was repugnant to a man who had trailed herds to Chicago, to Denver, to New Orleans, to Mississippi, without once having a barricade set against him. He reluctantly paid the toll, but he bequeathed his prejudices so strongly to Goodnight that to avoid tribute the latter decided to break a new trail from Fort Sumner to Denver. It lay over Trinchera Pass north of Capulin Volcano. This pass, previously unknown, was discovered by Goodnight. Decades later, the Fort Worth & Denver City Railroad established its line from Trinidad, Colorado to Des Moines, New Mexico, through Trinchera, climbing the volcanic uplift by an amazing feat of railroad engineering.

From Raton Pass Loving trailed his herd down to Trinidad on the Purgatoire River, a tributary of the Arkansas. The earliest Santa Fe traders in 1821 had followed this route. The Purgatoire (Purgatory) was named by French trappers a half century earlier, but its name had been corrupted to 'Picketwire' by the English-speaking traders and traildrivers. A few miles down the 'Picketwire' below Trinidad, Loving forsook the Santa Fe Trail and crossed over to the Aspishapa River. He was once more back in country which, were it not for the watercourses draining the eastern slope of the Rockies, would be a semi-desert. The rainfall on the plains from Trinidad to Cheyenne averages about twelve inches a year, including winter snows. Most of the streams carrying the run-off from the mountains are aggrading and soon lose themselves in the thirsty sandchoked channels. But what water there is, is fresh and potable.

Where the Aspishapa joins the Arkansas, Loving connected with the trail from Texas which he broke eight years before. He turned west up the Arkansas to Pueblo and the junction of Fountain Creek. The trail runs due north up Fountain Creek, almost to its source at the foot of Pikes Peak; thence across to the headwaters of Cherry Creek, which brought him into Denver.

Here Loving disposed of the remainder of the herd to John Iliff. Any story of the cattle industry in Colorado must begin with John Iliff. All of his stocker cattle came up the Goodnight Trail from Texas. Iliff's headquarters were at Julesburg. His range extended over a hundred miles along the Platte River, virtually from the mountains to southwestern Nebraska. It was thus through Iliff that Texas cattle fed the Colorado miners.

We return now with Charles Goodnight in 1866 after he left Loving north of Fort Sumner. Word of their success spread rapidly. He quickly gathered a second herd and threw them on the trail. He and Loving met at Bosque Grande, a fertile portion of the valley marked by a cluster of cottonwoods in a bend of the river, suitable to hold a herd all winter if necessary, forty miles south of Fort Sumner.

On this second trip, Goodnight found the solution to the problem of bringing a herd across the waterless stretch from the Middle Concho to the Pecos. He allowed them to graze to satiety before launching them onto the desert. After that they were grazed only briefly morning and night. Otherwise they trailed constantly, covering 95 miles in two and a half days and two nights.

Most of the obstacles man has overcome in his long, slow upward climb have been mental. Once Mount Everest has been scaled, the four-minute mile has been achieved, or the atom has been split, they no longer present barriers to the human mind. The impossible becomes commonplace. Actually Goodnight and Loving were not the first to take a herd across the dry drive. One of their cowhands, George Reynolds, who worked for Goodnight for years on this trail, and who became one of Texas' most successful ranchers, took a small herd across and up the Pecos in 1865. But the size of Goodnight's and Loving's operation and its well-publicized financial success fired the imaginations, hopes and ambitions of cattlemen all along the Texas frontier. There were many herds in 1867 following where Goodnight and Loving had led. The waterless stretch had been conquered.

Other complications developed, however. Horsehead Crossing was also on the trail used by parties of Quahadi and Penateka Comanches raiding the towns and haciendas of Chihuahua, Mexico. When these Indians discovered, as they promptly did, that vast herds of cattle were being driven from Texas up the Pecos, they promptly and methodically initiated plans to intercept these drives, so as to stampede and steal the cattle and horses. The Comanches had developed a flourishing trade in stolen Texas livestock, which they sold to the settlements and army posts in New Mexico through local traders known as Comancheros. Many of these drivers, including Goodnight, would arrive at Fort Sumner to find cattle carrying their brands being trailed in from the Texas Panhandle by Comancheros who had traded for them with the Comanches in the draws of the Llano Estacado. Suits instituted in the federal court in New Mexico to recover these stolen herds met with little success.

The Goodnight and Loving Trail was distinguished from all others in a number of respects. It presented many geographical obstacles to be overcome, as it crossed deserts and mountain passes. It was wide open for hundreds of miles to flank attack by both Comanche and Apache Indians. The route lay through wilderness, while the trails into Kansas and Missouri were through settled country where supplies were available. But the marked difference was that while the eastern routes were directed toward a railhead, the Goodnight and Loving Trail ended at the door of the consumer.

This trail became the third most important in the number of Texas cattle driven to market annually for the ten years from 1866 to

1875. About a fourth of all herds trailed during these years followed this route. The 10th U.S. Census reported that in 1874 there were 110,000 head driven to Colorado on the Goodnight and Loving Trail.

One pioneer whose name is indelibly linked with it was John Chisum, who is not to be confused with Jesse Chisholm for whom the Chisholm Trail was named. John Chisum came to Texas the year following the Battle of San Jacinto. He established a ranch in Denton County which became the largest cattle outfit in north Texas prior to the Civil War. He too, like Loving, was a beef contractor for the Confederate Army. At the close of the Civil War, in order to escape Reconstruction grief and "carpet bag courts", which Chisum regarded as a greater menace than the Indians, he moved his operations into the very heart of Comanche range in Concho County near the Colorado River. That he was able to protect his herds for years far beyond the reaches of the Texas frontier from the savage Comanche is a remarkable tribute to his courage, his resolution, and his ingenuity. He was not personally one of great traildrivers, but over 100,000 head of Chisum's cattle were driven by other trail bosses to New Mexico and Colorado. On Goodnight's second drive in 1866 he replenished cattle stolen by the Comanches through purchases from Chisum. In later years Goodnight trailed many of John Chisum's cattle from the Concho to Fort Sumner at a dollar per head profit.

Another early driver was John Hittson. He trailed many of his own and Chisum's cattle to feed Navajoes at Fort Sumner and miners in Colorado. His drives averaged from eight to ten thousand head annually over many years. In 1872 Hittson moved his stock to Deer Trail, Colorado, 50 miles east of Denver on Dijou Creek. Here he remained and became one of Colorado's leading cattlemen for many years. It is a mark of his versatility that prior to the Civil War he had a large plantation near Waco on which his numerous slaves raised cotton.

Thrilling tales of courage and adventure on the Goodnight and Loving Trail might be recounted endlessly. One incident is indispensable to the understanding of those simple virtues of loyalty to friends and devotion to duty which transcended all self-interest. On the 1867 drive Goodnight and Loving were late getting onto the trail because of Indians and other difficulties. While still below Pope's Crossing, Loving decided to push ahead to Fort Sumner to negotiate a sale. Several days later he and one companion were jumped by a large party of Indians, but found a precarious refuge under a bluff along the Pecos. They held the savages off until dark, though Loving received a shot through the arm which lodged in his side. By agreement, in the dark of the moon the companion, "One Arm" Bill Wilson, made his escape down the river to seek Goodnight, at least a hundred miles away. Loving realized the impossibility of his holding out until help could arrive, so he sought to make his escape upstream, and did so. He was found by several Mexicans and carried to Fort Sumner. Goodnight had searched the area and decided that Loving had either been killed or had drowned trying to escape. To his great astonishment he found Loving in the army hospital when he arrived at Sumner. Loving's wound in the arm did not heal properly and gangrene set it. An amputation by army doctors did not reach the infection and he died September 25th. His regret, as expressed to Goodnight, was at being buried in foreign soil. Charles Goodnight promised him that he would be laid away in the cemetery at home. After trailing the herd to Denver, Goodnight returned to Fort Sumner in the spring of 1868. He and his cowboys exhumed Loving's body and placed it in a casket they built. This was then secured to a wagon frame. With his cowboys riding behind and before, the funeral cortege proceeded back down the Goodnight and Loving Trail for Weatherford, Texas, more than seven hundred miles away. This must have been, by all odds, both in point of time and distance, the longest funeral cavalcade in history. J. Evetts Haley's poignant description of this touching incident says it all:

> Their arrangements were sufficient. Down the relentless Pecos and across the implacable Plains the journey was singularly peaceful. Through miles of grazing buffaloes they approached the Cross Timbers, reached the settlements, and at last delivered the body to the Masonic Lodge at Weatherford, where it was buried with fraternal honors.

In the uncertain scale of human nature, there is no standard for the computation of the influence of one noble soul upon another. Though Goodnight was then thirty-one years of age, until his death nearly sixty-three years later, he never spoke of Loving except in utmost tenderness, and his vibrant voice mellowed with reverence as he would slowly say, 'my old partner', and raise his eyes to the picture that hung on the ranch house wall.

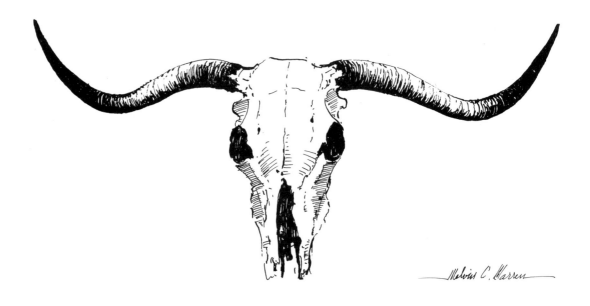

152

The Sketch Book

Illustrations by:
Melvin C. Warren

Back Down the Trail to Texas

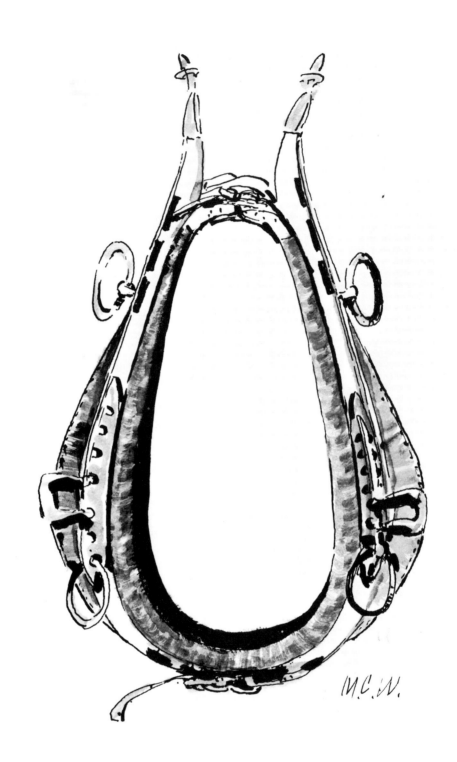

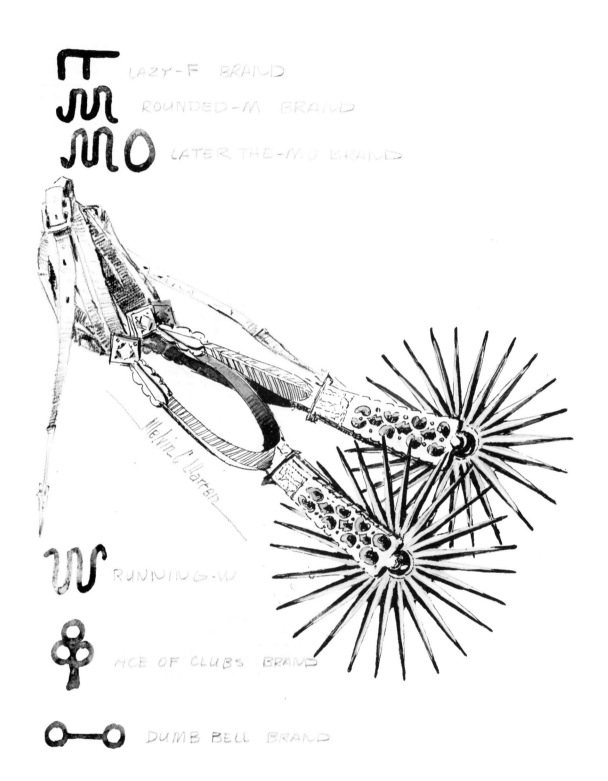

LAZY-F BRAND

ROUNDED-M BRAND

LATER THE-MO BRAND

RUNNING-W

ACE OF CLUBS BRAND

DUMB BELL BRAND

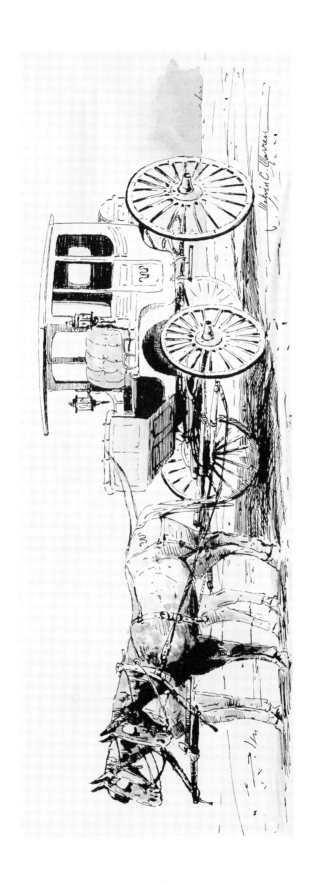

171

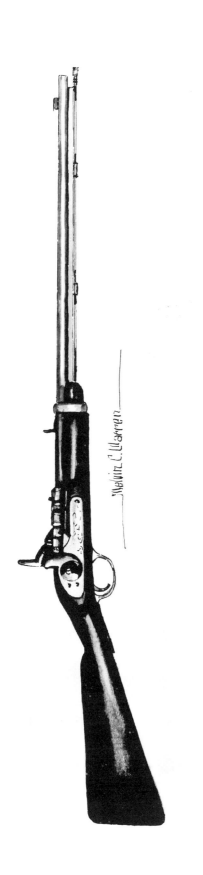

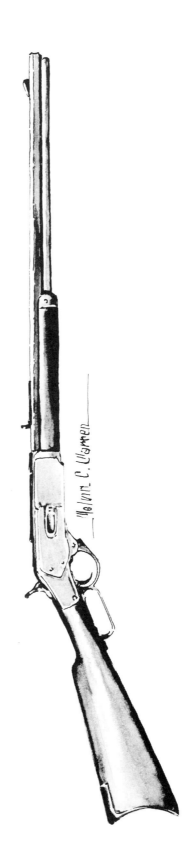